PERTH

Tradition & Style in Eastern Ontario

Tay Creek. (Ontario Archives)

PERTH

Tradition & Style in Eastern Ontario

LARRY TURNER

WITH JOHN J. STEWART

NATURAL HERITAGE / NATURAL HISTORY INC.

Published with the assistance of the Ontario Heritage Foundation,
Ministry of Culture and Communications.

To my ancestors who first set eyes on Perth, Edward and Benjamin James, Jane Godkin, Jane Kirk, William and Thomas Hicks, Benjamin Dickinson.

Perth: Tradition & Style in Eastern Ontario
by Larry Turner

Published by Natural Heritage / Natural History Inc.
P.O. Box 95, Station "O", Toronto, Ontario M4A 2M8

Design and typesetting: Robin Brass Studio
Printed and bound in Canada by Hignell Printing Limited, Winnipeg, Manitoba

Canadian Cataloguing in Publication Data
Turner, Larry
Perth : tradition & style in eastern Ontario
Includes bibliographic references and index.
ISBN 0-920474-75-6
1. Perth (Ont.) – History. 2. Perth (Ont.) – Description and travel. I. Title.
FC3099.P47T87 1992   971.3'82   C92-095183-X
F1059.5.P47T87 1992

FRONT COVER: *Gore Street, Downtown Perth*
BACK COVER: *The Tay River in Wintertime*
Both cover paintings are by Canadian artist Larry Bracegirdle.

The image of the Clock Tower is used courtesy of the Town of Perth.

Natural Heritage / Natural History Inc. gratefully acknowledges the financial assistance of the Ontario Arts Council and the Canada Council.

Contents

Acknowledgments

I am descended from three families in Perth, two of which resided permanently. The James family arrived from Wexford County, Ireland, in 1817 and settled nearby in Drummond Township, and the Hicks family arrived from Devonshire, England, around 1842. The Dickinsons, arriving in the 1880s, were also from Wexford, by way of Kemptville. My fascination with history was drawn from stories of their past and from the legacy of Pethern Point Cottage, the family retreat on Rideau Lake.

I remember being surprised, when writing a couple of term papers on various aspects of Perth history at Trent and Queen's universities, that so little had been published on such a colourful past and a living heritage. The opportunity for further research on Perth came when I wrote a history of the Tay canals for the Canadian Parks Service in the mid-1980s. In 1987 I became principal historian at Commonwealth Historic Resource Management Ltd., an integrated consulting firm that offers a full range of professional services directed at heritage resources. Jim Walsh, then on the town council, Doug McNichol of the Perth Museum, and publisher Barry Penhale at Natural Heritage/Natural History Inc. in Toronto encouraged the writing of a concise history; with financial support from the Ontario Heritage Foundation and time from my employer, this book is the result.

John Stewart and I have many people to thank. I was fortunate to have listened to Winnifred Inderwick, Peter (Gay) McLaren and Gordon Wilson before their passing. I never had the opportunity of meeting the late Eric Sabiston, Edward Shortt, Archibald M. Campbell, James Kinloch, John Kellock Robertson, and W. T. L. Harper but appreciate their abilities to collect and save important aspects of Perth history. Peter Code and Ronald 'Rusty' White are treasure troves of local lore and legend, and Rusty allowed me access to his wonderful scapbooks on Perth business and sports. Judge John Matheson was very helpful on military history. I have enjoyed discussing Perth history with several individuals including Susan Code, Hugh Halliday, James De Jonge, Doug McCalla, Elwood Jones, David Roberts, Bob Passfield, Bob and Marian Sneyd and many others. I have enjoyed contact with three historians who have helped shape our understanding of chain migration and kinship in the cultural foundation of eastern Ontario, Bruce Elliott, Glenn J. Lockwood, and Marianne McLean.

I interviewed by phone or in person, Murray Quattrochi and Angelo Rubino, Dick McVeety and Ned Winton, Mary Rogers and Willa Shortt, Peter Moskos and Jim Kanelakos, Désirée Girouard, Steve Fournier, Ron Rutherford, Ken Barr, Doug Cavers, Hilary Fowler and many others offered information on their businesses or families. Eli Hoffman, Laura Armstrong, Stuart M. Douglas and several others provided photos and documents. I have also enjoyed the support of Steve Forster and Michael Taylor of the Perth *Courier* where several local articles were published. My colleagues at Commonwealth, including Hal Kalman, Jamie Silversides, Fern Graham, Ian Hunter, Jim Graham, Rhonda Stewart, Sandy Crozier and Arlyce Shiebout have been helpful in many ways and I enjoyed collaborating with John J. Stewart on several subjects and appreciated the time that was granted to pursue this project. John also wrote parts of this book on Perth's architectural significance and would like to thank Margaret Archibald for reviewing his contribution. The publisher, John and I appreciated support from the Ontario Heritage Foundation, especially Paul Bator. We also appreciate the careful attention given to this project by Barry, Jane and Nancy Penhale, editor John Parry, artist Larry Bracegirdle, and designer Robin Brass.

LARRY TURNER
Commonwealth Historic
Resource Management Ltd.
53 Herriott St., Perth, Ontario
June 1992

Introduction

Perth has always been an enigma. It has had a curious history with regards to business opportunity, investment climate, and transportation linkage. A large portion of the town's early elite was made up of professionals, half-pay officers, and civil office-holders. Capital flowed in from the public purse, but it did not "stick," except in genteel homes and prominent facades. Several general merchants and artisans developed important local networks in business and trade, but in manufacturing there has been limited investment in and identification with the town.

Perth had several jump-starts: military stewardship, 1816-22; cash from half-pay officers in the original settlement; appointment as district town, 1823; building of the Rideau Canal, 1826-32; appointment as county seat, 1850; a railway boom and new canal in the 1880s; and the economic leadership pf John A. Stewart, 1900-20. Early in the twentieth century Perth attracted an unusually diversified group of companies manufacturing felts, pharmaceuticals, cosmetics, shoes, and textiles; later it was making as well components for machinery, paper products, cutlery, batteries, and other products. Perth's most distinctive industry, the two home-grown distilleries known for their whiskey, were destroyed under government legislation in 1916.

Like other eastern Ontario towns, Perth had small mills, tanneries, foundries, carriage and furniture factories, and artisan's shops. It had a tradition of service and commercial industries such as banks, law firms, insurance companies, hotels, groceterias, and merchant houses associated with a market and administrative centre. Except for the Code Mill on Herriott Street and the distilleries and mills using water from the Tay River, most plants were on the outskirts of town, while the commercial and service sector gravitated to the centre. This pattern of development protected the core from industrial expansion, and it preserved a unique and attractive downtown.

Perth has always been just a little off the beaten paths, a few miles from the main Rideau Canal, for several years at the end of a branch railway, a couple of miles from the highway, a little isolated, a little different. Its insulated character is still revealed in the high expectations of its architectural surround. It was a small frontier centre thrust into a large wilderness tract.

Perth did not happen naturally. It was imposed on its site- an administrative centre for an inland military settlement almost like a garrison, with enough re-tired officers and limestone to make it feel like one. In 1823, it was made centre of administration for the Bathurst District, a wilderness of struggling pioneers, yet it was located on a watershed that could not sustain widespread development. Perth was located on a small river, not a mighty water-power like Almonte; it was on a branch canal, not like Smiths Falls on the main canal; its first railway was a cul-de-sac, not on a trunk line as in Carleton Place. Perth had to forge its own character beyond its very ordered and public origins. Its very obstacles to progress are a key factor in the survival of its distinctiveness.

Perth was the invention of government. The pattern of assisted emigration and military settlement defined its instant status as a military depot. For many years after the original diaspora between 1816 and 1822, Perth tried to forge a commercial network, as well as maintain its central administrative function within the Bathurst District. When the field of endeavour started to diminish after 1850, and boundary changes saw a reduced role as to county seat, competi-tion from other rising centres challenged Perth's original hegemony. The town faced limitations that it was not prepared to accept. Based on the early expecta-tion of its inhabitants, an overwhelming concern of its residents for half a cen-tury was the means by which Perth could reassert its influence over the surround-ing area and subsequent immigration. The character of Perth is reflected in this nineteenth-century challenge: to make itself look as important as it thought that it should, almost as a denial of what it had become – a small, self-conscious Rideau Valley market town, service centre, and modest-scale manufacturing site, with county-wide responsibilties in local government.

The characteristics of nineteenth-century development can still be detected in many small Ontario towns. Where "progress" has meant change, growth has often obliterated what stood before. If we can read from the past through surviv-ing structures and artifacts, as well as letters and diaries, then Perth is a book with many rich leaves.

This volume is a concise history designed to pull together the major facets of Perth's origins and development. It offers a structure for interpretation and ex-ploration. If the material generates debate and discussion it will have served its purpose in stirring, rather than solidifying the pot. It is a history in progress, where the field of play is still broad and the horizon endless. The available primary resource material in newspapers, diaries, and manuscripts is rich in variety and extent, and this snapshot of Perth is a mere overview of a tapestry where each thread is a complex story in itself. It is a building block.

This history seeks to explain why Perth happened and how it developed to be what it is today. I have refined the story to concentrate on patterns of settlement, the development of the town, and the role of transportation in growth and lack thereof. I assess the contribution made by religious and educational institutions as well as the military tradition that helped shape the town. I discuss Perth's identity through cultural transfer and homegrown character, in relation to the pursuit of leisure and recreation. As well, John J. Stewart looks at the formation of Perth's particular ethos through its architectural symbolism and setting which were significant in the development of Perth's tradition and style.

CHAPTER ONE

A Military Settlement

The Rideau Military Settlements

The Rideau military settlements were born out of concern for the defence of Upper Canada from invasion by the United States. The War of 1812 had revealed the vulnerability of the thin line of settlement along the St. Lawrence River between Montreal and Kingston. British military authorities and colonial leaders agreed that survival would depend on the reinforcement of St. Lawrence settlement patterns with the population of interior corridors. In hindsight, the Rideau corridor would have succumbed to the human wave that was immigration from the British Isles in the nineteenth century, but the original settlement at Perth was designed to direct people to an unsettled interior against the conventional wisdom of land-seeking immigrants. This end was accomplished through government-sponsored military settlement and assisted immigration.

The original townships surveyed for the Rideau military settlement in 1816 were not even located on the Rideau Lakes or Rideau River but were part of the watershed located in Bathurst, Drummond, and parts of Sherbrooke and Beckwith townships. The lands through which the Rideau coursed were largely part of an 'empty frontier' owned and controlled by United Empire Loyalists who had originally settled in the St. Lawrence townships in 1784 and who had received interior properties in lieu of rewards for their service in the American Revolutionary War. Loyalists, their descendants, and later purchasers were absentee landlords, awaiting incentives to develop or sales on speculation. As a

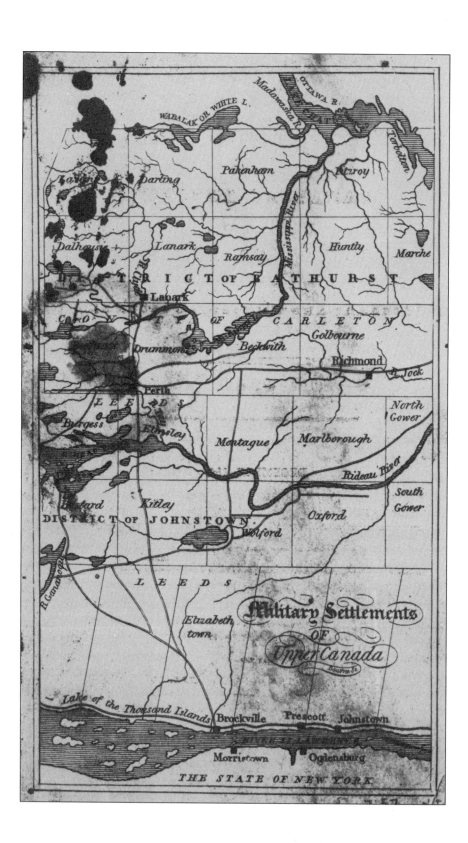

group, the Loyalists and their families were granted over three million acres of land in Upper Canada. Governor General Lord Dalhousie at Quebec would lament in 1820 the "useless waste" of large grants made by governments "which they can neither recall, nor force into settlement," creating "a serious difficulty in the way of prosperity of this part of the Country."[1]

The Rideau corridor was not completely barren before the War of 1812. Some early Loyalists trekked north to the Rideau River at Burritt's Rapids and Merrickville and other small clearings, but there were two larger settlments near the Rideau in the rear of Leeds and Grenville County. In 1794 Samuel Stafford of Saratoga Springs, New York, attracted 24 people to Marlborough, Montague, Oxford, and Wolford Townships, where 408 inhabitants were residing in the "Rideau settlement" by 1803. Also in 1794, Abel Stevens brought 200 Baptists from Vermont to settle in Kitley and Bastard townships.[2]

Most settlements were determined by quality of land, waterpower, and access to existing or potential means of transport and communications. Perth was imposed on the Tay River as a military depot in 1816. Surveyors and officials took into account environmental factors such as the riverside location and the lay of the land, but theirs was a quick, unnatural process for determining potential. The location of Perth, especially as a central depot, made little sense. If the military sought to hide Perth in the corridor, then they were successful. Given the availability of land and the short time frame for planning and surveying, it was perhaps the best possible site on the Tay River, the largest of the Rideau's small, regional arteries. But Perth was several miles from the natural line of a proposed military canal, and a more suitable location would have been the mouth of the Tay River, now Port Elmsley. However, at the Tay mouth a large tract of land was owned by the Arnold and Weatherhead families from the St. Lawrence. The same problem existed for other sites at rapids further downstream on the Rideau.

For occupying and taking control of the land, military settlement was perceived as an effective tool in organizing civilians as well as soldiers after the War of 1812. This attempt to control migration reflected concern by post-war government that Upper Canada had to adhere to established British principles and authority. Upper Canada, it was thought, would be better able to defend itself against the chaos of republicanism from internal and American threats with a loyal settlement of British soldiers and civilians.

(Facing page) Perth was district town of the new Bathurst District (created in 1822) but located near the southern boundary with the older, established Johnstown District. The role of district town enhanced Perth's early prominence in eastern Ontario. Perth, Lanark, and Richmond Settlements, 1824 (Scale: 8 miles to an inch) William Bell, *Hints to Emigrants* (Edinburgh, Waugh and Innes, 1824). (National Archives of Canada (NA), NMC 15,712)

The Rideau military settlements were part of an ambitious plan for defence of the Canadas, including fortifications at Montreal and Kingston. On the Rideau system, the three-point plan included eventual development of an inland waterway between Kingston and the Ottawa River to ensure a military supply line; settlement of loyal British immigrants to ensure civilian resistance to invasion; and placing of discharged British soldiers among the civilians to protect the planned waterway and settlement. While the government was experienced in military resettlement, it had no precedent to follow in assisted emigration.

The War of 1812 had exposed weakness along the border and within the colony. There was concern that a settlement pattern based on the "ill disposed and disaffected settlers of American origin" who had been coming to Upper Canada for the three decades following the American Revolution threatened British authority. Americans supposedly brought with them republican ideas and notions of equality that did not conform to British ideals. By restricting American settlement, the colony, it was hoped, would avoid traitors and disaffected citizens which had become a serious concern during the war. There was growing realization, as well, that Britain was exporting too much of its population to an American adversary. A scheme was therefore hatched to divert British emigrants to Upper Canada, where they would form a loyal bulwark among the settlers of American origin. The Colonial Office devised assisted emigration, which in 1815 had nothing to do with creating a desirable outlet for a redundant population but was premised on defending the Canadas.[3]

While a settlement of loyal civilians would form one part of the scheme, the British already had a large number of soldiers who had been fighting Napoleon in the Peninsular Wars and Americans on the border with Canada. With the ending of hostilities on both fronts, the government was wary of disbanding excess soldiers, only to have them return to Britain where post-war recession and unemployment would be severe. In order to reward the fighting force with grants of land, to alleviate unemployment at home, and to form a core of loyal ex-soldiers who could form militia units on new lands, Britain set up the Rideau military settlements.

Assisted Emigrants from Scotland

Lord Bathurst became colonial secretary in Britain just as the War of 1812 was declared. His idea for assisted emigration received an enthusiastic response in 1813 from Lieut.-Gen. Sir Gordon Drummond, administrator of Upper Canada, who stressed the need for settlement in eastern Ontario. Although there was still opposition in Great Britain to the promotion of emigration, the government justified assistance on the basis that people were leaving anyway, and this should be turned to Canada's gain.[4]

In 1817, Mary Black Bell (1773-1861) travelled for 12 weeks from Scotland to Perth while pregnant and caring for 7 young children. Her husband, Rev. William Bell described "inconveniences and privations" in his diary, but we have no interpretation from her. (Courtesy Perth Museum)

Hoping to send 2,000 settlers from Scotland and 2,000 from Ireland, as well as a number from England, the government in February 1815 released details of its plans which included the generous offer of free passage and provisions on the voyage, 100 acres of land, six months of rations, and agricultural provisions at cost. Public support of a school teacher and minister was included in expectation of the people's settling as a community. The important rider was the requirement of a deposit, £16 for each male over 17 years and £2 for each married woman, refundable after two years of actual settlement. The deposit was steep enough to discourage most of those who might be interested, and it satisfied British opponents of the promotion of emigration. It was also designed to prevent settlers from skipping over the border on arrival in Canada.[5]

The deposit restriction kept numbers down to 699, about half from 48 parishes in the lowland vicinity of Glasgow as well as adjacent areas in the western borders and near Edinburgh, on both sides of the Firth of Forth. The other half came from four parishes in the Highlands, especially in the Breadalbane area of Perthshire and the Glenelg area of western Inverness-shire.[6] Lord Bathurst had a distinct preference for Highland settlers, and there were few Irish or English respondents, owing to advertisements being restricted to Scottish papers. The program was also cancelled early, owing to renewed hostilities with France after Napoleon's escape from Elba in 1815.

The emigrants found that transatlantic resettlement, whether funded privately or publicly, was tedious and complicated. Owing to the war alert, transports were late in arriving, and the *Atlas, Baltic Merchant, Dorothy,* and *Eliza* left Scotland between 11 July and 3 August 1815. The settlers would arrive in Canada too late to look after themselves, and they would spend a miserable winter waiting in barracks at Brockville, Cornwall, and Fort Wellington, while a number took employment in Kingston. For some, loss of their deposit was not a disincentive for leaving the migration.[7] For others, the isolated Rideau did not seem appropriate for settlement. A petition from Scottish settlers at the end of 1815 complained:

> The petitioners will humbly state the reasons which make them reluctant to settle on the Rideau, and likewise the inducements they have to proceed up. The crops in the Rideau are subject to hurt from early frosts; the lands are badly

watered for cattle, at an immense distance from the St. Lawrence, and no water conveyance for their wood and produce. These are the reasons which chiefly pre-possess them against the Rideau. To these, allow them to urge the advantages of the Upper Country — a great superiority of soil and climate, a much longer sea-son for carrying on farming operations, and many other smaller advantages appear of incalculable advantage to them...[8]

While these observations were remarkably astute for newly arrived immi-grants, they were based on real concerns about inland settlement, away from the mainstream of commerce and trade and running counter to conventional wis-dom, which encouraged settlement in fertile areas being opened further west. Resentment by American-origin residents along the St. Lawrence to the intru-sion of British settlers who would change the character of the community may have also discouraged the arrivals. However, given the condition of the land that many would come to possess and the long-term problems of interior communi-cation, the unsolicited advice may have been sound.

There were among the Highlanders families who had been promised settle-ment near their kin in Glengarry County, and an exception was made to allow for their staying in the St. Lawrence River region. They settled into townships that would become Lochiel and Kenyon, leaving only 12 percent of the High-landers heading to Perth. The division split the original Scottish contingent in two, with slightly more than half staying in Glengarry. The bond of kinship and community enabled the Highlanders to bend the government's original inten-tions. The Military Settling Department almost wavered in favour of allowing the settlers reserves near the Bay of Quinte, but by March 1816 the Rideau mili-tary settlement at Perth was beginning to take shape.[9]

Military Settlement

While plans were made for demobilizing soldiers as early as 1813, it was not until the beginning of 1815 that details were released. The soldiers had been promised a land option if they did not wish to return home. The deal included 100 acres of land free of fees in a military settlement, a year's provisions, and necessary farm implements. The land could not be sold until after three years of occupation and cultivation. Officers were originally restricted to 200 acres, to keep the settle-ment compact, with subsequent land granted according to rank, with lieutenant-colonels allowed up to 1,200 acres.

The military settlers were British Regulars who had served in Upper and Lower Canada during the War of 1812, soldiers recruited for home service in Fencible units from British North American colonies, and officers of the army and navy who had not necessarily served in Canada but had declared their intention to reside there. They were a colourful collection of veterans from European and North American theatres of war, of many different backgrounds and levels of experience. While the officer class enjoyed extra land, town lots, half-pay pensions, and the familiar hierarchy of their military bearing, soldier-settlers were more likely to be transient, especially if single, and quickly alienated from the task of clearing and establishing a farm.

The Military Settling Department, which was responsible to the commander of the forces in the Canadas, administered both civilian immigrants and soldier settlers. The surveying of land and the passing of patents were entrusted to Upper Canadian officials. In fine bureaucratic tradition, the appointed officials fought over prospective locations, surveying duties, and other details. The largest problem was how to settle the soldiers and civilians along the Rideau corridor when most of the land had already been alienated. The military refused to scatter the settlers on crown reserves through the tract and insisted on a concentrated settlement. The eventual compromise led to settlement north of the Rideau system, rather than enveloping the lakes and river.

Sir Gordon Drummond, as commander-in-chief and administrator in Lower Canada, as well as the immediate agent of the Colonial Office, argued with Lieutenant-Governor Francis Gore in Upper Canada over the eventual location of the settlement. Although Gore and Drummond streets today run parallel in Perth, such was not the case in the two men's perception of settlement. However, by March 1816, a party was sent to find a potential location for a government depot northwest of the Rideau system. It was led by Lieut.-Col. Francis Cockburn, deputy quarter-master general to the forces, who from Quebec directed much of the affairs of the Rideau military settlements.[10]

In February 1816 the crown signed a treaty with the resident Algonkian Indians for tracts of wilderness lands north of the Rideau system. Surveyor Reuben Sherwood located the townsite on the Pike (later Tay River) instead of at a location formerly agreed to at Jebbs Creek near Otty Lake. Alexander McDonnell, a former Loyalist officer in the Royal Highland Emigrants and superintendent of the Rideau military settlement, sited the land for a government storehouse by the Tay River in order to receive 30 loads of provisions by late March. Col. Christopher Myers, a deputy quarter-master general, reported the settlement of Perth commencing on 18 April 1816. Weary settlers began arriving by way of wagon road, ox-cart, and scow from Brockville via Delta, Big Rideau Lake, and a portage from Beveridges Bay to the Tay River. The surveys of land were late, but newcomers were alotted properties as soon as possible, and those wishing land in the village obtained town lots of an acre each and were set to building houses.[11]

Swiss Regiments

A colourful attachment to the military settlement in Perth consisted of two Swiss regiments, de Watteville and de Meuron. They were part of several Swiss regiments organized in their native cantons which served as auxiliaries in allied countries. From 1801 the Regiment de Watteville had been part of the regular establishment of the British Army, and it had served in Malta, Elba, Egypt, Italy, and Spain before being sent to Canada in 1813. Louis de Watteville, the colonel-proprietor and financier, was at the head of 41 officers, 1,414 men, 8 servants, 45 wives, and 38 children as they made their way to Kingston to serve in the garrison. While all the officers were Swiss, as well as several soldiers, the contingent was made up largely of Germans, Hungarians, Italians, Poles, and Russians, along with some Greeks and French. They were professional soldiers, mercenaries, and even some captured men from Napoleon's armies. The regiment engaged in combat in the Niagara Peninsula, and in 1815 Louis de Watteville was promoted to commander-in-chief of the armed forces in Upper Canada.[12]

The Regiment de Meuron, formed in 1781, served originally with the Dutch before transferring to British service in 1798. It had served in India, Gibraltar, Malta, and Sicily before being sent in 1813 to Canada where it was involved in the attack on Plattsburg and did garrison duty in Montreal.

After the War of 1812 was over, soldiers who so desired were allowed to take up land in military settlements. However, the Swiss regiments were quickly dispersed: land surveys at Perth were not ready in time, and there were attractions elsewhere. As officers like de Watteville returned to Europe, the familiar leadership was lacking at Perth, and few ex-soldiers took up land; of those who did, fewer than 40 percent stayed on their property long enough to acquire patent. Approximately 150 de Watteville settlers were located at Perth, and about 22 de

The Reverend William Bell (1780-1857) photographed in August, 1848. The Presbyterian minister described by his biographer as "a man austere" arrived in Perth in 1817 to start a mission, open a school, and impose the moral policing of the Kirk-session on his new congregation. His letters and diaries provide an invaluable portrait of life and society in Upper Canada. He described this photo being taken for the first time in his life in a diary entry for August 1848. (Courtesy Perth Museum)

Meurons. The Perth-area settlers were mostly Swiss, German, and Polish. Among the Canadian Fencibles were some who made up Perth's "foreign legion" in new settlement.[13]

These regiments contributed ethnic variation and gastronomic diversity. In *Recollections of the American War, 1812-14,* Dr. William Dunlop commented on some of the de Watteville soldiers: "though they could not equal the Canadian Militia in woodcraft, they greatly excelled them in gastronomic lore; and thus, while our fellows had no better shift than to frizzle their rations of salt provisions on the ends of their ramrods, these practical botanists, sent out one soldier from each mess, who gathered a haversack full of wild pot herbs, with which and a little flour their ration was converted into a capital soup."[14]

Early Arrivals

Some of the first houses of Perth were covered with boughs or bark until log cabins could be carved from the forest. The Scotch Line, running along the border of Bathurst and Burgess townships, amidst a fertile clay plain, was a favourite location: "Scattered along the Line and hidden from one another by the surrounding woods, stood the rude homes of these pioneer farmers, each in the centre of its own little clearance. They were ... log houses chinked with moss and plaster, with troughed roofs generally, a low door in the south side, and one or two small square windows, cut in the thick wooden walls."[15]

In the fall of 1816, Col. Myers reported 20 houses being built in the village, 250 homes in the immediate vicinity ready for occupation by winter, and 1,505 people in the area: 840 men, 207 women, and 458 children. A visit to the settlement by Sir Francis Gore on 7 October 1816 led to an appeal for continued support for the settlers until they could care for themselves. The particularly cold summer of 1816, caused in part by the eruption of Mount Tambora on the Pacific Ocean, and combined with the magnitude of clearing wilderness lands, left many settlers in need as winter approached. In 1817, the Reverend William Bell reported 1,890 residents, with discharged soldiers and their families outnumbering civilians by more than two to one: 708 soldiers to 239 male immigrants.[16]

As first missionary to the settlement, Rev. Bell was greeted warmly, and he made interesting observations:

> 24 June 1817: After a long and fatiguing walk, an opening appeared among the trees, and Perth was announced. The situation appeared to be pleasant, being on the banks of the Pike River, now called the Tay. Not more than 30 log buildings were then erected, and most of them small. Without loss of time, I waited upon Captain Fowler, with my letters of introduction. He was very civil and introduced me to the other officers of the settlement – gave me at once a park lot of 25 acres, and a building lot in the village, and took me home to dinner.

25 June: In the evening a wagon arrived with Mrs. Bell and the family, when we took possession of a house which we had rented a year, for £20 near the west end of the village. It had no furniture and we had to spread our bed upon the floor, but we were glad to find ourselves at the end of our journey, and to have a house we could call our own. Twelve weeks travelling, with a family of six [seven] children, the oldest not yet fourteen, it may well be supposed had subjected us to many inconveniences and privations. Some of the children had suffered so much from the mosquitos, coming through the woods, that they were almost blind for some days after their arrival.

29 June: As it rained all day, few of the country people came in, no proper roads being yet opened. I preached at 11, and again at 2, to about 30 people, including the servants of government, and a few half pay officers. I could see that, in discharging my duty here, much patience and caution was necessary. The people were much in need of instruction, but the most of them were careless about it. The moral as well as the natural world seemed to be a wilderness.

2 July: Today I visited all of the families in the first two miles of the [Scotch] line, and met with a cordial welcome at every house. Their huts, or shanties, were mostly poor, but the improvements they had made upon their land, in one year, were much to the credit of their industry. Most of them had from two to eight acres cleared, and under crop (...)

9 July: The rations to the settlers, from the government store, being all this time stopt, and many of them left the settlement, chiefly of the discharged soldiers. At 2, our meeting on church affairs was held, in the school-house. I observed with regret that some came bare-footed, and very poorly clad. The poverty of the people prevented any thing being done at this meeting, beyond appointing a committee.[17]

In 1817, the Scottish radical Robert Gourlay visited Perth; he so displeased the ruling elite of Upper Canada that he was banished from the colony in 1819. His purpose had been to write a statistical account of settlement for British emigrants, but after his visit to Perth he decided to inquire into the conditions of all other settlements in the colony, to the embarrassment of the upper crust. On 15 September 1817 he wrote an open letter about the Perth settlement, which contained only mild criticsm (he was saving his venom for the half-pay officers later), and it appeared in his *Statistical Account of Upper Canada* (1822): "I diverged from my route about fifty miles, and spent some days at Perth, situated on the waters of the Rideau, to which a considerable body of the people, who accepted the invitation of government, had been conducted. Here I traced the reported discontent to some neglects in the general management, and some ill conceived petty regulations, capriciously exercised towards people tenacious of their rights; but in the main, universal satisfaction prevailed among the settlers, and a strong feeling of the good intention of government towards them."[18]

The Military Mystique: A Lasting Legacy

A garrison mentality was at the core of Perth at its beginning. The town attracted not just foot soldiers but a large portion of ex-officers drawn by land, half-pay pensions, and the opportunity of continuing the familiar hierarchy of the officer class in a new society. Winnifred Inderwick listened intently to the stories that she heard as a child:

> But after all, Perth was very important, Perth and York people were all intermarried and interrelated. It was the only real military settlement in Canada, you see, and it was very, very snooty. They always said you had to be in Perth twenty-five years before you were accepted into society. You always went to dinner according to your rank. In this house [Inge-Va] that would have happened and that protocol was very closely observed. By the same token, they didn't have too much money, you know. They were half-pay officers and they usually went through that pretty fast, I think. I might see an officer's wife out helping her husband dig potatoes in the morning, but at night she would go to dinner in a fashionable evening dress, London-made. It might be about ten years old but it was quality.[19]

Early settlers included a colourful array of soldiers and officers who could talk about fighting in the Peninsular War under Wellington or battling the Americans at Crysler's Farm and Lundy's Lane. There were some from the Swiss regiments with experience fighting under Napoleon. They came from an astonishing range of regimental formations and origins, documented by J.A.B. Dulmage in "Origins of the First Settlers" in *Perth Remembered*. They included members of the Royal Volunteers, Royal Artillery, Royal Navy, Army Service Corps, cavalry units, a wide range of regiments of the line, and colonial militias. There were two different Glengarry Light Infantry regiments, one from Scotland and the other from Upper Canada.[20]

As a military settlement created from fears and doubts about a fragile border, Perth was expected to be a focus for settled militiamen who could be readily mustered to defend the province. Although many ex-soldiers, especially the unmarried, left the settlement before putting down roots, those who remained were active in the militia. Militia musters among ex-soldiers, officers on half-pay, civilian settlers, and their growing sons became an ingredient in the early social fabric of male activities.

A militia commission was considered a mark of status, given a large stable of officers on half-pay readily available for service. At least 63 non-commissioned officers settled in the Perth district. It is not surprising that Perth's military elite would relish militia activities nor that early leaders such as Donald Fraser, Henry Graham, Anthony Leslie, Alexander McMillan, and Josiah Taylor were also landowners, merchants, or magistrates.

The upper ranks of the new militia strove to meet high expectations, but the rank and file would gather annually with few weapons and little in the way of uniforms. Militia day was an excuse for "the boys" to gather for some games and frolic. Unfortunately, some of the games included recreational violence, especially on militia day in 1824, when the 4th Carleton militia and Irish immigrants did battle. Irish Protestants and Irish Catholics with short fuses and long memories had strong opinions about the penal codes and the insurrections of 1798 in the old country, and scores had to be settled in the new.

Rev. William Bell reported much "drinking, swearing, and fighting" on these militia days: "June 4th being the training day for the militia, the town was full of men, and music, noise, and nonsense. Most of them came in, up to the knees in mud and water, the road being very bad, but to prevent them taking cold, at least the usual quantity of whiskey was drunk. There were horse races on the streets, too, to the terror of mothers, and the danger of all."[21]

Perth was part of the 2nd Regiment of Carleton militia in 1821, and the name was changed to the 2nd Regiment of Lanark in 1825 (the county of Lanark was created in 1824 out of the county of Carleton in the Bathurst District). William Morris was named first lieutenant-colonel of the Perth wing in the militia, a position that he held for more than 20 years. In 1826 the regiment had 692 rank and file. A Lanark Artillery Company, known also as the Perth Volunteer Artillery Company, was raised and attached to the First Lanark Regiment in 1826. There was no shortage of interest, since 39 of the settlers had once served in the Royal Artillery.[22]

The militia was called out during the Rebellions of 1837-38, and men and the artillery were sent to the St. Lawrence on three occasions. Lieut. Hogg, Perth Artillery, wrote a poem on one tour of duty at Fort Henry in Kingston: "Fort Henrys proof-ramparts her bull-dogs displaying / Well mann'd with stout hearts from Perth upon Tay."[23]

In November of 1838, colonels Alexander McMillan and William Morris of the 1st and 2nd Lanark Regiments, respectively, published a broadside in Perth and several outlying townships telling militiamen to be ready. The tone of the message reflected the deep-seated fear of American invasion, and the call to arms harkened back to the Rideau military settlements original role as a bulwark behind the frontier:

> We feel it our duty to apprize you that another attempt to invade these Provinces, is about being made by numerous bands of lawless citizens of the United States associated with disaffected persons who have left this country. The chief object of those who thus menace the peace and security of the unoffending inhabitants of Upper Canada, is plunder. No man's property will be safe. Rapine and bloodshed will mark

the progress of those diabolical disturbers of our quiet homes. The destruction and subversion of our Government and Constitution, however dear to us, are only accompaniments of the main object of the wicked Banditti, whose intention is to seize the property of every loyal man, as a reward to this horde of Pirates.

If we are true to ourselves, they can do us no harm. The resistance of an indignant injured people, will soon drive them from our soil. Be ready then to march to the frontier at a moment's notice, should your Captains receive orders for that purpose. – Put your affairs in such a state of arrangement that no delay can take place when you receive the call, – and let our movement be cheerful, prompt and determined; with such feelings animating a loyal people, the period of service can be but a few days, for the invaders of our soil cannot maintain a cause so unrighteous.[24]

In 1846, the militia was reorganized, with Perth forming the 1st Battalion, Lanark, of the Regiment of the Bathurst District. Roderick Matheson, a sergeant in the Canadian Fencibles and a half-pay officer in Perth, who had been quarter-master of the Glengarry Light Infantry Fencibles in the War of 1812, was promoted to lieutenant-colonel. Change came again after the Militia Act of 1855, when Matheson was given command of the 1st military district of Canada West, a position that he held until 1863. The American Civil War and the threat of Fenian raids heightened tensions after mid-century. About 1866 another reorganization saw Perth companies (both Company No. 3) created in 41st Brockville Battalion of Rifles and the 42nd Brockville Battalion of Infantry. The name of the local militia was changed in 1897 to the 42nd Lanark and Renfrew Battalion of Infantry, and again in 1900 to the 42nd Lanark and Renfrew Regiment.[25]

The Perth Guns[26]

Symbolic of Perth's militia role, and of that of the Rideau miltary settlements, are the two historic field guns that protect the Court House Green given to the town in 1820. They were built by Dutch-born master founders Jan and Pieter Verbruggen of the British Royal Brass Foundry in 1775 and 1776. Both are three-pounder light-infantry guns constructed in the "Galloper" tradition of the 1740s: the smaller is a General Pattison "grasshopper," the only known surviving gun of its kind; the other is a General Townsend "butterfly" (also known as Congreve's three-pounder or Light Common three-pounder). The guns were cast as part of the armaments to accompany Gen. John Burgoyne and the British Army in 1777 on his raid from Canada to divide the rebellious colonies along the Hudson River-Lake Champlain axis during the American Revolution.

What happened next is a mystery. Were they used by Burgoyne? Were they kept in storage at Quebec? Research by R.V. Manning and J.D. Chown of the Canadian War Museum has eliminated the story that the guns were captured by the British from the French in Holland. However, there is some substance to the theory that the guns were lost by Burgoyne at the surrender at Saratoga in 1777 and recaptured by the British at the Battle of Crysler's Farm during the War of 1812. Since the guns were built for Burgoyne, who was soundly trounced by the Americans, he may have lost them to the victors. It is known that brass cannon, including four at Bennington and six three-pounders at Saratoga, were taken by the rebels. Some of these cannons were used by the Americans in the War of 1812, but at Crysler's Farm in 1813 the attackers were using mostly six-pounders and few cannon were captured.

Several Perth settlers fought at Crysler's Farm. Colonels Fraser and de Hertel; Captains DeLisle, McKay, and McMillan; Lieutenants Blair, Matheson, and Watson; and at least seven privates bore the memories of that famous defence of Canadian soil. They were eye-witnesses and either saw the guns captured or, when two cannon arrived in Perth a few years later, evoked a myth that would give the guns some meaning and significance.

In 1820, Lord Dalhousie, governor-in-chief of the Canadas, requested that the two guns be sent to Perth, as well as armaments to Richmond and Glengarry, to "applaud and encourage" the miltary spirit in the new settlements and "induce them to form volunteer companies." It had the desired effect, and a Perth Artillery Company was formed around the two guns, which arrived about 1824.

Dalhousie had thought that the guns would be useful for the "particular purpose of assembling the inhabitants in celebration of His Majestys birthday and other such festivals." The Perth Artillery Company did not disappoint. The guns belched forth on royal birthdays and for special events such as the inaugural voyage of the steamer Enterprise on the Tay Canal in 1834. A 23-round salute was pounded out on 12 August 1837, when Queen Victoria was proclaimed monarch. The artillery company withered, but John Manion, son of a Crysler's farm veteran, maintained the tradition until 1888. On occasion, the guns were used as a percussion device to raise drowned bodies from local lakes. They were hauled all the way to the battle site of Crysler's Farm in 1895 for the unveiling of a monument.

Whether captured at Crysler's Farm or not, the Perth guns are part of the legacy of remembrance. The Hicks carriage factory donated new wheels in 1912, and they were restored by the James Brothers Foundry in 1924. After blacksmith Sam Kelford of the Scotch Line restored the two cannon in 1981, an attempt was made to move them to a museum, safe from environmental elements. Reeve Norman Turner led the crusade to return the guns to their traditional locations in 1982. The guns are an important part of Perth's symbolism and setting. They evoke the military origins of pioneer settlement and the role of the militia in defending the country, and they serve as a landmark in the collective memory of the community.

CHAPTER TWO

Half-Pay and Sandstone

Perth has long been recognized as a gem in the heritage landscape of Ontario architecture. Few communities have been able to protect their generational identity like Perth, where landscape and architecture have evolved and meshed to create a small treasure of a town. Much of the credit for Perth's cultural landscape and the quality of many of its homes and public buildings – mostly made of local sandstone – can be traced to its location. Perth is situated on a sandstone deposit: it resembles an island and has produced a very distinctive environment. For settlers, readily available, high-quality, and easily workable sandstone underlay a fertile soil, supporting abundant stands of black walnut, butternut, oak, cedar, and white pine. Even a few miles north and west, the Laurentian Shield tapers off, and the land is rocky close to the surface, offering little agricultural promise for the pioneers who settled there.

Perth was selected as the main depot of the Rideau military settlements for strategic reasons. The townsite was well drained, on slightly higher ground overlooking a river, with good farmland nearby. Although swampy in parts, the river was expected to serve as a transportation conduit and afford power for grist and sawmills. Although the location proved less than ideal for military purposes, settlers found the site very suitable.

Equally important to an understanding of Perth's character is the settlement plan which organized the town according to a prototype designed and instituted by Lord Dorchester in 1789, for inland townships in Upper Canada. When

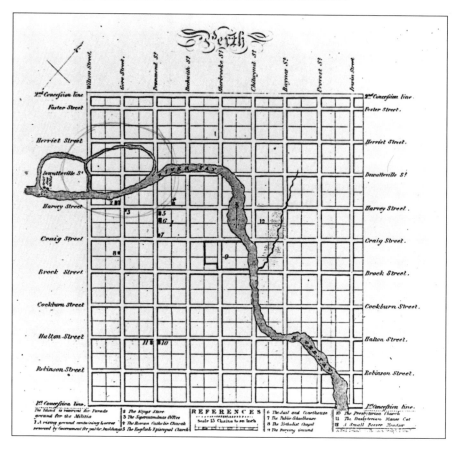

The 1816 survey plan for Perth straddled the Tay River at odd angles to the compass. Four one-acre building lots formed each block. The streets were named after contemporary governors, military officers and surveyors. William Bell, *Hints to Emigrants* (Edinburgh, Waugh and Innes, 1824). (Courtesy Louis Melzack Collection, Fisher Rare Book Library, University of Toronto)

Reuben Sherwood in 1816 imposed his gridiron pattern on the townsite of Perth amid the wilderness, he introduced the Georgian rationalist sense of order which carried through to a plan organized around a hierarchy of sites. The highest point of land was reserved for public buildings. Is there any surprise that the Court House and attendant jail and registry office would be flanked on one side by the Church of England and Ireland, and on the other by the 'Auld Kirk,' the Church of Scotland? Both churches sought establishment status and ascendancy in Upper Canada, and both had to be content with sharing with others the Protestant field. The Roman Catholic church for a few years attempted to share the same hill, but later moved to a site where the spires of St. John's soared above all.

The town straddled the Tay River, which imposed its own geometry on the rigid grid, introducing a 'romantic' or 'picturesque' flavour to the engineered system of four-acre blocks and streets. Perth was laid out at odd angles of the compass. The river meandering through the centre of town contributes to one's perception of Perth and the sense of place. A series of stone arched bridges connected parts of the town. Reinforcing the experience is one of Perth's most distinctive landmarks, Stewart Park, a gift to the town in 1925 from the Stewart family and developed as a public park in 1947. Abutting the park are Code and Haggart parks, at the corner of Herriott and Wilson streets. These two areas in the centre of town bridging Haggart and Cockburn islands form one of the most pleasant town park systems anywhere.

Perth was sardonically referred to as "the half-pay officer's paradise." Town lots of one acre were reserved for officers, thereby dictating the development of individual properties and buildings in Perth. Several half-pay officers or administrators and lawyers, drawn to the town by its status as district town, encouraged expectations in dwellings as reflected in the surviving Summit, Inge-Va, and McMartin houses, as well as such properties as Rock Cliff cottage, built on lands owned by Dr. Thom in Carolina Village; all were erected before 1833.

The organization of lots and the street pattern established a visual order for buildings and their relationship to the streets. This vista-creating axial planning is apparent in such buildings as Drummond Vue, the Sneyd residence at the foot of Drummond Street, and St. John's Roman Catholic Church, at the foot of Brock Street. The focused view of the rapids and the arched pedestrian bridge from Herriott Street is another delightful play on axial planning. As well, the Georgian urban ideal for the placement of buildings prevailed, and despite the very large lots most dwellings were situated close to the street – even later in the century, as speculators subdivided lots and houses were constructed.

Building materials were never a problem in Perth, blessed with stands of oak and pine, located near beds of limestone and sandstone, and adjacent to a clay plain that provided ample mortar and ingredients to make brick. A part of the uniqueness of Perth's architecture is the local cream-coloured Potsdam sandstone or freestone and a reddish-tan variety as well. Early travellers judged a community by its ratio of brick and stone buildings to those built of wood. The first stone structures in Perth were built by Scottish masons. Among the earliest settlers on the Scotch Line were two stonemasons and a ship's carpenter. With skilled masons and the easy availability of local sandstone, stone construction was under way even before the Rideau Canal brought a second wave of experienced tradesmen into the area. Rev. Bell pointed out that three brick buildings and the first stone one were under construction in 1823 in *Hints to Emigrants*, written for consumption in Scotland.[27] In 1846, the *Canadian Gazetteer* noted "The jail and court house is a handsome building of white freestone; and the town contains several good buildings of stone and brick, and one or two ornamented with white marble, which may be procured in any quantity within a few miles of town."[28]

Builders were not a problem to find. Lieut. William Blair of the Glengarry Light Infantry Fencible Regiment established a brick factory in 1816 on his lot in Bathurst Township. After the opening of the Rideau Canal in 1832, experienced stonemasons from Scotland, and probably Ireland and England as well, contributed their skills to early buildings.

Perth was an instant town, designed to serve as a depot and administrative centre to an inland military settlement. In the familiar grid pattern, broad streets cut the town into blocks of four building lots of one acre each. The lines on the land imposed an immediate symmetry, a system of control, made all the more glaring with the unimaginative naming of the town and river after ancient places in Scotland. Unlike many town plans in Upper Canada that fronted a river or lake, Perth straddled the Tay River, which was expected to serve as a conduit to the local district. The river actually impeded growth in the town, with the original centre being located in the East Ward around the king's stores, the superintendent's office, and the four acres reserved for public buildings on the rise of ground dominated by the court-house.

Planners anticipated growth in the West Ward, above the 2nd concession line, or North Street, where they set aside sixteen 25-acre park lots, although this site had not been within the original town boundary. The cluster of park lots set aside for men of means and station was a way of engineering the type of growth that could be expected when the "right kind" developed these sites. Of the sixteen park lots granted, at least eight went to half-pay officers, which reinforced the military presence in the new town.[29]

The Rev. William Bell noticed that while soldiers settled on farms, most of the officers were attracted to their lots in town:

> The whole number [of officers] amounts to between 30 and 40 and most of them are justices of the peace. This gives them a greater influence in the settlement than is perhaps agreeable to the civilians, few of whom hold commissions of the peace, or any other office under government ... instances of arbitrary and oppressive conduct may have occurred yet in general they have conducted themselves with a degree of moderation and politeness that does them credit.[30]

Early in the settlement, the half-pay officers monopolized government positions and dominated the social structure. They included numerous magistrates and the earliest businessmen, and they organized the first militia companies. At least £5000 of half-pay income and pensions amounted to an infusion into local hands in 1820. When one considers that the assistant superintendent and store-keeper was paid £182 a year, this cash flow, while not all concentrated in Perth, was a substantial infusion of capital in a developing community.[31]

A former Presbyterian minister, Rev. James Ross, suggested in an article of reminiscences in the Perth *Courier* on 30 June 1905 that the roots of Perth's sluggish growth can be found in its original settlement: "Many of the early settlers were men with a pension or on a stated income, which they quietly enjoyed, and they seldom took risks in the way of investment. To this has been attributed that strange lack of enterprise which dwarfed the town at the period during which it ought to have grown, so that its small neighbours passed one by one."[32]

Robert Gourlay's *Statistical Account of Upper Canada* (1822) condemned ex-soldiers in Perth and other military settlements: "soldiers, in general, choose their trade only to indulge in idleness, and give reins to a roving disposition; and after having 20 or 30 years in the profession of gentlemen, cannot easily train into the habits of sober and perservering industry."[33] However, Gourlay was even more critical of the officer class, especially in Perth, as stunting general growth through private speculation:

> ... Captain Fowler [superintendent of the settlement at Perth after Alexander McDonnell] actually offered me a thousand acres of land if I would settle at Perth; and on my objecting to the lots lying asunder, "O!" said he, "that is more in your favour, as it becomes valuable from the efforts of the other settlers;" and here indeed is the secret. It answers very well, indeed for half-pay officers to get their 500, their 700, and their 1000 acres so located; because not one in ten of them ever cultivate their land, and if not intermixed with the farms of the poor settlers, it would never bring them a farthing. The officers let their land lie waste in lots of 100 acres or 200 acres all over the country in this way, till, by the efforts of the industrious, it fetches money to them, the drones. This is the way that Canada has been impoverished, first and last...[34]

Even military superintendents Alexander McDonnell and Daniel Daverne at Perth could not keep their hands off the largesse being offered, with McDonnell being relieved of his post for speculating in 1816 and Daverne escaping the country with supplies in 1819. Some of the earliest businessmen and entrepreneurs, however, were half-pay officers.

There was widespread resentment in the pioneer community for the influence and power wielded not only by the half-pay officers but by the entire establishment at Perth. A public notice posted by Daniel Shipman about 1824 called for a meeting:

The Inhabitants of the County of Lanark are requested to attend a Meeting.... To take into consideration the importance of selecting Fit and Proper Persons as Candidates for the next ensuing Election, as it is of great importance to prevent improper persons, – such as Merchants, Lawyers, Half-pay Officers, and Nobility from imposing themselves on the great body of inhabitants; – experience teaches us that these form no part of the Domestic Agricultural Body of our Inhabitants, therefore they may be considered as having no practical knowledge of the local situation of our country, consequently cannot entertain just views of its Policy to Redress the Grievances under which the great body of inhabitants at present labor.[35]

The Richmond and Lanark Military Settlements

Richmond amd Lanark military settlements soon joined nearby Perth. The Perth settlement encompassed primarily the townships of Bathurst and Drummond, parts of Burgess and Elmsley nearest to Perth, and portions of Beckwith and Sherbrooke. As the western half of Beckwith Township opened up, some Scots and Irish emigrants who arrived in 1816 and 1817 ventured east from Perth. In 1818, a second military depot was established on the Jock River in southeast Goulbourn Township and named Richmond, in honour of the new governor-general, the Duke of Richmond. This locale resettled men from the 99th Regiment who chose to stay in Canada. Most were from the western Irish counties of Ulster who had been raised for colonial service as the 100th Prince Regent's County of Dublin Regiment. As well, Irish Protestants from North Tipperary, headed by Richard Talbot, settled in Goulborn, and a number of Perthshire Highlanders in Beckwith. A persistent inflow of Wexford- and Carlow-area Irish Protestants balanced the original Scottish character of immigration with a rising tide of Irish families seeking to put a troubled past behind them.[36]

When the Colonial Office launched assisted emigration in 1815, the purpose was the defence of Canada. Later, until such schemes were largely abandoned in that form by 1822, the goal was relief from post-war depression, especially among handloom weavers, and homes for displaced tenant farmers from the Highland clearances. With the recognition of overpopulation in the British Isles, emigration was no longer seen in negative terms. In the words of Thomas Malthus in *Essay on the Principle of Population* (1817), "The only real relief in such a case is emigration; and the subject is well worth the attention of the government, both as a matter of humanity and policy."[37]

The Lanark military settlement, set up in 1820 north of Perth, involved military supervision of civilian settlement. In 1820, Glasgow-area weavers and mechanics began to band together in emigration societies, petitioning government to convey them to the colonies. Under pressure from Scottish lords and MPs, a package was proposed that would provide a free land grant of 100 acres, survey expenses, seed and implements at cost, and an initial capital loan of £10 per head, if the emigrants would pay their own passage from Scotland to Montreal. The first shipment of 167 families, consisting of about 840 emigrants, embarked in 1820 and was followed by almost 1,900 people in 1821. In the latter year, 32 societies numbering 6,281 individuals sought to emigrate, but the government forced a reduction of almost two-thirds. The Lanark settlement was supplemented with about 700 Scottish immigrants who had come out on their own and some discharged soldiers.[38]

The Lanark settlers were tenacious. Of 569 heads of families who occupied lots in 1820-21, 544 were still on their land in 1829 and 403 remained in 1834. Owing to the original deployment of Scots in the Perth area, the emigration societies insisted on land nearby. In consequence, they were settled in the townships of Lanark, Dalhousie, North Sherbrooke, and Ramsay, later described by Sir John Colborne as "the worst tract of land on which any extensive settlement was ever attempted in Upper Canada." [39]

While Scots arriving in Perth are well documented during the years of military supervision, 1816-22, many Irish Protestants also settled in the area. Between 1816 and 1822, 1,006 Irish arrived in the Rideau military settlements, and half located in and around Perth. Approximately 20 percent of Irish immigrants arriving at Quebec were heading to the region, the vast majority from the southeastern province of South Leinster, including the counties of Carlow, Kilkenny, Wicklow, and especially Wexford.

Declining economic opportunities, continued sectarian strife and apprehension, and positive letters home from earlier settlers north of Brockville led Protestants in Leinster to envision a more secure future among familiar faces in distant lands. Without any government assistance, but with the kind of internal family and community support that characterized chain migration, Protestants from this region and others helped settle the Perth area. Immigration increased for many years after the military superintendency was abolished.[40]

J. A. B. Dulmage, in *Perth Remembered*, suggests that England and Ireland contributed a higher proportion of the ex-soldiers than Scotland.[41] Rev. William Bell commented in 1817 that there was a mistaken impression in Scotland that Perth was inhabited chiefly by Scots. He pointed out that there were people from all around Europe, the majority of them discharged soldiers, but Scots settlement had clung largely to the stretch of clay plain south of the Tay River (the "Scotch Line"). Since the discharged soldiers were generally the first to arrive and the first to leave, early ethnic composition was affected by the departure of soldiers and increased immigration from the British Isles. Approximately half of the soldier-settlers abandoned their lands before receiving a patent. The civilians were more persistent, with about 70 percent receiving patents, and that permanence in settlement was linked more closely to having a family than to having good land.[42]

The Colonial Office ceased to support assisted emigration in the manner of Perth and Lanark. While the original Perth migration was inspired by colonial considerations, Lanark's resulted from domestic concerns in Britain. The Military Settling Department provided necessary provisions far beyond its mandate, to help immigrants before they could take up their land and after they had settled. There were problems of accountability, especially when assistant superintendent Daniel Daverne absconded with funds and supplies at Perth. The government advanced Lanark settlers £22,724, most of which it never saw again because of poor conditions for farming. Although the Lanark settlement was better organized than Perth's, and included some of the hardiest and most persistent settlers, it could hardly sustain itself on the land on which it was placed.

In December 1822, the military settlements were handed over to civilian control, except in Lanark, which was extended for one more year. The areas in 1822 had 10,763 residents, 3,570 of them men; of these, 1,307 were discharged soldiers and 2,263 immigrants. The Military Settling Department had located most of these people, almost all of whom were from the British Isles, but for Europeans in the Swiss and other regiments and a handful of Americans. Except for some British North Americans in the Fencible regiments, all were relatively new to Canada. Only a small group of Irish and English settlers had found their way to the settlements via the United States.

The Rideau military settlements shaped the development of Perth. The town became the gateway to much of the new settlement, especially to its immediate north. As an instant service centre, Perth could hardly manage its own growth, let alone sustain a hinterland just bursting with development. One can imagine the first years of life in Perth not unlike that of a small gold-rush town. For the first six years, at least a thousand men, women, and children, with all their baggage and accessories, would wind their way through pioneer trails each spring and early summer, to arrive spellbound, at a rough-hewn shanty town by the Tay. From miles beyond, horses and oxen would bring in farmers needing basic goods. In 1823 all the houses were built of wood, except a courthouse, jail, and merchant's store built of brick; the first stone building, a tradition of which Perth would become justly famous, was under construction. There were seven merchant's stores, five taverns, four churches, and between 50 and 100 houses.

CHAPTER THREE

District Town

The District of Bathurst, created in 1822, consisted of lands along the Rideau River system northward from the Johnstown District, including present-day Ottawa. It was a massive tract of land that would become Carleton, Lanark, and Renfrew counties. In 1823 Perth was named district town.

Perth had been created suddenly in 1816, and it anchored the Rideau military settlements. Within a short time, it was servicing a wide agricultural and resource frontier in several nearby townships north of the Rideau system. The potash industry, associated with the early clearing of land, was Perth's first major export, along with lumber, wheat, and butter. General merchants such as half-pay officers Henry Graham and Roderick Matheson, and former Brockville resident William Morris, set up commercial facilities to service a hinterland. Indeed Perth's military men were its first business people – not surprising considering their incomes. Visitors marvelled at the transformation of Perth. In 1820 Rev. George Jehoshaphat Mountain wrote:

> The settlement of Perth, so laboriously reached, affords one of the most encouraging examples of the kind that I have seen. It appears hardly credible that, less than four years ago, it was a portion of the wilderness, unexplored except by the wandering Indian hunter. Streets were laid out, and the building lots occupied, in some instances, by very good and neat houses; two places of worship erected; gardens and farms under cultivation, and yielding abundant returns; a very tolerable society, enjoying the intercourse of civilized life; and everything wearing the aspect of cheerfulness and competence; – such is the scene which the skill and in-

Looking down a raw Gore Street in 1828 past where the Town Hall stands today. To the left, the original Roman Catholic and Anglican churches, the old Court House and James Boulton's Summit House dominate the highest point of land. Sketched 20 August 1828 by Thomas Burrowes. (Archives of Ontario, sketch no. 22)

dustry of man have carved for him so quickly out of the depths of the trackless forest.[43]

By 1823, Perth had seven general stores; in 1830, Joseph Bouchette described it as a "thriving village" of 350.[44] Its status as gateway to outlying settlements made it much more important than its population would imply. Perth's umbilical cord was tied to the St. Lawrence River and Montreal, a connection reinforced after completion of the Rideau Canal in 1832. The canal also opened up the Ottawa Valley trade to the north and the expanding American market via Kingston, Oswego, and New York's Erie Canal to the south.

Establishment in Perth of administrative offices for the new Bathurst District in 1823 meant more extensive development of services such as taverns, hotels, and livery stables to handle people visiting on official business. The town attracted an elite minority of professionals and administrators such as lawyers and magistrates who injected capital into the economy and in turn created demand for substantial houses, consumer items, and services. By 1846, this public sector included judge of district court, sheriff, clerk of peace, inspector of licences, crown lands agent, judge of surrogate court, registrar, district clerk, clerk of district court, superintendent of schools, and deputy clerk of the crown. This collage of individuals gave the frontier town a genteel, self-important face.

Behind the Facades

James Boulton (1801-1878), Daniel McMartin (1798-1869), and Thomas Mabon Radenhurst (1803-1854) were sons of distinguished parents and were well on their way to becoming prominent in Upper Canada when they became Perth's first three lawyers. They were educated by Dr. John Strachan (1778-1867), a teacher of society's leaders at the famous Cornwall and later Home District Grammar schools, and they arrived as young lawyers to forge new careers in the district town. Each man left a permanent statement of his aspirations on the face of the town, and their differing styles of architecture reflect deep-seated division in taste and sentiment. Their rivalry affected their colleagues and community, and the last fatal duel may be attributed in part to the tension between them.[45]

James Boulton was the son and brother of assemblymen, solicitors general, and attorneys general of Upper Canada. At the age of 22, he was the first lawyer to arrive at the new district seat in Perth in 1823, and he immediately erected the town's first brick home, the Summit. The house represents blendings of two architectural traditions, one from Toronto and the other local. The main influence is the five-bays, two-storey Georgian house with low hipped roof, as in the Toronto homes (both demolished) of "Family Compact" members Bishop John Strachan and Attorney General John Beverley Robinson and the surviving "Grange," built by D'arcy Boulton (James's brother) in 1817-18 and the Campbell House, erected by Chief Justice Sir William Campbell in 1822.[46]

Members of the Boulton clan were at the top of "a privileged few" in Upper Canada's establishment. They were transplanted British gentry comfortable within the prevailing, conservative ideology of the governing elite, where family, class, and patronage held sway. They were charter members of a small group of officials (the "Family Compact") who dominated the legislative and executive councils, the judiciary, and senior bureaucratic positions in government. James Boulton would build himself a house that reflected his perceived stature. It was meant to show the people of Perth his social and political pedigree, as well as his sophistication. Of

Daniel McMartin (1798-1869), the son of a Loyalist captain, was born in Williamsburg, near Cornwall. He arrived in Perth as a new barrister of law in 1823. He quickly gained prominence with a clientele that stretched east to Ottawa and north to Renfrew and Pembroke. He built his ostentatious house on Harvey Street in 1830. (Archives of Ontario, Acc 10449)

course, the Boulton house, perched on Perth's highest incline, sat next to the seat of local power, the Court House.

Unlike the Toronto mansions, the facade of the Summit has no projecting central bays, and the roofline is broken not by a classic pediment but by a gable which is not perfectly aligned with the windows below. The changes suggest use of local contractors and introduction of aspects of a local house type being developed in the Rideau Valley, in which the front or main-facade roofline is interrupted by a central gable over the main door. The typical Rideau Valley house, however, is only one and one half storeys high and is built of stone or wood. So the use of brick and the full second floor are features that Boulton brought from Toronto.

The second Perth lawyer was the ostentatious Daniel McMartin, son of a Cornwall-area Loyalist officer in the King's Royal Regiment of New York and brother of an assemblyman and the sheriff of the Eastern district. He built an elaborate brick house trimmed with marble in the "Loyalist" or "Federal" style in 1830. It has been described as one of the most pretentious homes in Canada, sporting three lanterns or belvederes on the roof. The "extremely linear, knife-edged and complex" house reflected the personality of its owner. Although the house did not lord over the settlement like Boulton's, McMartin's pile did announce his presence quite effectively.[47]

Inge-Va, an eastern Ontario landmark erected for Rev. Michael Harris in 1823 and later the home for the Radenhurst and Inderwick families. The Inderwicks donated it to the Ontario Heritage Foundation in 1974. (Photo by author)

The Federal-style McMartin House (1830), was later owned by the O'Brien family, and it was purchased by Lanark lumberman Boyd Caldwell as a wedding gift for his daughter Mary Jane as she married William Grant, a Perth physician. The building has served public purposes for most of this century and is now a senior citizens' meeting place owned by the Ontario Heritage Foundation. (Photo by author)

Enter a year later, in August of 1824, the "Father and Champion of Reform" in Lanark, Thomas M. Radenhurst. He married his cousin, a daughter of Thomas Ridout, an assemblyman, legislative councillor, and surveyor general of Upper Canada. Unlike his Tory counterpart, Boulton, and in spite of his Ridout in-laws, he was a Reformer and a friend of Robert Baldwin. They were opponents of the "Family Compact" who wished to see the ruling oligarchy displaced by responsible government which would give more power into the hands of electors. Radenhurst did not build, but moved into by 1832, the gracious, late Georgian, neo-classical stone house known as Inge-Va,-Tamil for "come here" -erected in 1823 by the Reverend Michael Harris of the Church of England.[48]

Where the Summit traces its lineage to the homes of Toronto, and the McMartin to American models, Inge-Va is truly anchored in the Rideau Valley. Described affectionately by its third owner, conservationist Winnifred Inderwick, as "Country" Georgian, the stone house has a storey-and-a-half, end-gabled, centre-hall plan and is an early prototype for dwellings commonly built along the Rideau corridor. The Radenhursts introduced the dormer over the centre door and thus completed the form used over and over again for houses throughout Upper Canada. It would seem appropriate that the Reform-thinking Radenhursts would enjoy the progressive statement that their house made to the community.

Perth's young legal fraternity was a volatile mix. McMartin was described as always being at loggerheads with Boulton, and their backgrounds coloured their actions. Boulton was the youngest son of an upwardly mobile English family that brought with it a belief in a distinct order of class and place in society. For the Boultons, a backwoods ruffian like McMartin, born in the country, even if educated by the eminent Dr. Strachan, did not have the same station as true-bloods such as they. Daniel McMartin was described as a "keen, shrewd man who dearly loved a fight and who would neither give nor take quarter." Imbued with the frontier legacy of his family in both New York and Upper Canada, he had been brought up with a sense of achievement acquired by the hard work of a pioneer. It was also alleged that he built his home solely out of materials from the United States. To him, Boulton represented all that was wrong in privileged circles, where English blood and pedigree, not necessarily actions, defined class and status.[49]

Radenhurst, with his perceived dangerous radicalism was an enemy of both Boulton and McMartin. Radenhurst was recognized "for his strict integrity and professional pursuits" and represented Reform thinking which saw Tory privileges, whether earned or inherited, as an instrument of abuse. Not only was Radenhurst Anglican, however, he was a student of Strachans! The three social climbers hated each other with a passion. Had their dislike for each other stayed within the elegant confines of their mansions, few would have noticed, but their brawling and insults spilled out into public quarrels, horsewhippings, and beatings in the street. Several times they wanted to kill each other. They almost did.

In 1827, McMartin challenged Boulton to a duel; the latter declined, claiming, "he had no chance of hitting his opponent, he being no thicker than a broomstick." In 1830, Radenhurst dragged Boulton to the ground, the latter admitting "that my conduct on that occasion did not entitle me in much commendation." Radenhurst and Boulton agreed to a duel in New York state, but, as Rev. Bell commented, "they expected to have the pleasure of shooting one another without molestation. But this like all former affairs of the same kind ended in smoke."[50]

On 7 June 1831, Bell described Boulton and McMartin at it again, with Boulton horsewhipping McMartin, followed by a scuffle on the street. In April 1833, McMartin distributed a printed broadsheet calling Boulton "a liar, a coward, and a scoundrel."[51] In his reply to the public, Boulton revealed the deranged sense of honour associated with duelling:

If duelling is any proof of courage, (which I deny), I have provided that I am no coward by having given the satisfaction required by the laws of honor to a gentleman, to whom I had given cause – to call me out. But is there any reason because I choose to fight a duel with a gentleman, that I am to meet every low insignificant scoundrel, that chooses to have his feelings wounded, because his body is bruised, when he brought it on himself; no, ... It is possible he [McMartin] may work himself up with a little dutch Courage, to the determination of fighting a duel, but that will not restore his honor. Duelling is permitted in most countries, and I believe in this as a means, when there is no other address, to protecting character, not of redeeming it when lost.[52]

The duel of honour was a game of Russian roulette. It was a primitive form of justice that settled disputes of honour with the skill of marksmanship. It was a trial by ordeal where the "just" person would win. It was bloody brinkmanship at its worst.

Precedents for duels were few and far between, but in Perth, they were acceptable behaviour for gentlemen. In 1817, Samuel Ridout, Radenhurst's brother-in-law, fought a duel at York with John Henry Boulton, James Boulton's older brother. Then there had been the New York duel between Perth's Radenhurst and Boulton. Early in 1833, two half-pay officers, surgeon Alexander Thom and Alexander McMillan, fought a duel wherein the doctor was slightly injured, but "the matter terminated amicably."[53] Radenhurst was McMillan's attendant. Thom was Boulton's father-in-law. This duel, and the others, so close to the events of the last fatal duel, as well as Boulton's defence of the process, had to have had an effect on the students then studying under, and living in the homes of, Boulton and Radenhurst. Ultimately the family feud between the Radenhursts and Boultons would be settled by substitutes, once and for all.

The last fatal duel is now a part of Canadian folklore. In Perth it came to a tragic end on 13 June 1833. Robert Lyon, student at law under Radenhurst and related by marriage, fought with John Wilson, a student of law under James Boulton, over an alleged slight to the character of Elizabeth Hughes, not yet Wilson's girlfriend but later his wife. Lyon had sug-

A silhouette of Robert Lyon, c. 1830. He was the victim of the last fatal duel in Upper Canada on 13 June 1833. The duel was not an isolated incident, but rather a harsh form of male pride, frontier justice and elite bravado that came to a tragic end. (Courtesy, Perth Museum)

gested that Miss Hughes had allowed young men to indulge in little freedoms that were unbecoming. Lyon was carried lifeless to Radenhurst's house, and the following day, Radenhurst, described by Rev. Bell as mad with liquour, "had been running about the streets and through all the rooms of Mr. Boulton's house, with a pistol in his hand, seeing Mr. Boulton to shoot him." Boulton paid a high price for the conduct of his student. In 1833 he was hounded out of Perth as a result of "having made himself many enemies."[54]

The impact of Perth's first three lawyers is still strikingly evident today. The three homes of this early legal elite; Boulton's Summit still commanding its view over town; McMartin House still vigorously on display on the main street; and Radenhurst's Inge-Va in its refined, park-like setting, reflect differences in design and attitude. The three homes are symbolic of different trends in Ontario architecture; the buildings are recognized as provincial historic sites and two of them are owned by the Ontario Heritage Foundation. The Summit, McMartin House, and Inge-Va not only represent the highest ideals of architecture in Perth but tell a story about pioneer passion, social division, private competition, and Perth's notorious last fatal duel. As well, they tell the story of entrepreneurial spirit, long standing commitment, and love for one's community.

Agricultural Service Centre

Developing farmland on the clay plains near the Scotch Line and other fertile areas turned Perth into an agricultural service centre for a wide area in the Bathurst District. As trees fell and fields blossomed, the self-sufficient characteristics of pioneering agriculture changed swiftly with rising exports. Wheat, flour, butter, lumber, potash, and furs dominated the hinterland trade into mid-century.

Self-sufficient farm families in and around Perth could supply themselves with the necessities of life. Mary A. B. Campbell described the provision of clothing by women and travelling artisans in the home:

> Food and clothing were very expensive for many years, and such of the latter as could be bought at the small stores of the village was not very often such as would meet the requirements of a new country. All whose means would admit of it had brought from the old land a good supply of warm and comfortable clothing suited to the climate and the rough work to be undertaken, but when this gave out they had to depend on the resources of the new country. As soon as sufficient land was cleared to enable them to have sufficient pasturage for sheep, they were procured, and when the time came for their fleeces to be shorn, the wool thus obtained was washed, picked, carded and spun by the good wives on their little wheels, which had been brought out from their old homes. This wool was then woven into durable homespun by some of the emigrants who were weavers from Scotland and had their looms with them. The men wore gray homespun for rough working suits –

with brown for gala days – while the women and girls had gray flannel proms and skirts, with ones of checked woolen goods woven into tasteful patterns for better occasions. The dyeing materials used were mostly of nature's providing, golden rod making a fast yellow ... while hemlock boughs made a pretty brown and sumach a soft gray. The men wore linen shirts of home spinning, sometimes checked blue and white ones for working. All the better suits were made by a tailor who went from house to house to ply his trade.... A shoemaker always came once a year to every home, going from house to house carrying his tools and implements...[55]

Increasing revenue from the land and the growth of transportation encouraged consumer and commercial trade. The opportunities in Perth resulting from building the Rideau Canal and the expanding hinterland are visible in the operation of W. & J. Bell, general merchants. After having served apprenticeships under original merchants William Morris and Roderick Matheson, William and John Bell, twin sons of Rev. Bell, started their partnership in 1828. The Bells were merchants, speculators, commission agents, outfitters, and forwarders based in Perth. Like several other general merchants in town they were the intermediary between imports and exports going to and from Montreal. The Bells advanced credit in the form of goods to their customers, who sold their produce to the Bells,

John Haggart Sr. (d. 1854) of Breadalbane, Scotland was a stone mason and contractor who built Chaffey's Locks on the Rideau Canal and purchased the mills of Alexander Thom on Haggart's Island. A cluster of mills and the Haggart-Shortt residence were erected before 1840. The mill pictured here was built after a fire in 1841 and was eventually turned into a roller flour mill by his son, John Haggart Jr. (1836-1913). The mill was destoyed by fire in 1964. (Archives of Ontario, Eric Arthur Collection, 24 A2/2)

Local currency, also known as scrip or "shinplasters." The commercial crises of 1837-38 made coins and money scarce, and so William and John Bell made change until 1839 with their own notes in five denominations. Montreal artist Adolphus Bourne designed these handsomely printed notes, which served as a local medium of exchange. The 12 pence note pictures the old Bell store, which stood on Foster Street, near Shaw's, until 1901. (Courtesy Bank of Canada Museum, Ottawa)

who in turn paid off their advances of general merchandise from Montreal suppliers with the accumulated production of country labour. Debt was a critical feature in pioneer society and while the farmer was most dependent and bore a high risk, even the merchants suffered the consequences of economic crises.[56]

The Bells produced fractional currency in five denominations during the commercial crisis of 1837-38. Their handsome notes, designed and printed by Aldolphus Bourne in Montreal, were shinplasters which allowed them to make change when specie was scarce. Their distinctive notes were the first in Upper Canada and copied by several other merchant houses elsewhere. They remained in use until 1839, when they were withdrawn in the face of local and legislative pressure. The original plates are preserved by the Bank of Canada, and notes can be seen in the Perth Museum.[57]

The Bells recovered from the commercial depression and built their own barge, the British Queen, for use between Perth and Montreal. However, deep lines of credit to fur traders, lumbermen, and farmers, and their own debts to Montreal commercial houses, strangled the business. After the early deaths of William in 1844 and John by 1846, the company faltered during another economic crisis in 1846-47. The Bells had once imagined a fleet of their own barges using the Tay and Rideau canals. Six of the seven sons of the Rev. Bell were at one time clerks or owners of general stores, but with the loss of William and John, the dynasty was robbed of its mercantile twins.

Chain Migration

Lord Bathurst had realized in 1815 that if the settlers were satisfied with the conditions in which they found themselves, they would send letters home and "do more to create a preferance for Canada over the United States than any encouragement that the government could give."[58] In chain migration, original settlers influenced friends and family at home, who then joined their contacts as individuals, clusters, and even communities. Letters home were clearly the inducement for later settlers to locate in Perth and district. Three books published in Scotland in the early 1820s gave examples of such letters. Robert Lamond's *A Narrative of the Rise and Progress of Emigration from the Counties of Lanark and Renfrew to the New Settlements in Upper Canada* appeared in 1821; John M'Donald's *Narrative of a Voyage to Quebec, and Journey from Thence to New Lanark*, in 1823; and Rev. William Bell's *Hints to Emigrants In A Series Of Letters From Upper Canada*, in 1824. These accounts, as well as personal letters home, formed a crucial incentive for many to follow.[59]

Not all the letters sent from Perth were positive. Duncan Campbell, who had fled from "that place of poverty" to Caledonia, New York, by 1818, was accused by Peter McLaren of sending false reports about Perth. Campbell defended himself: "You would wish to send the good and not the evil. But I stated things fairly as they was, sending the evil as well as the good."[60]

The Perth area was infilled by settlers drawn to the area through settlement schemes, by word of mouth, or by means of public works such as the building of the Rideau Canal. Irish Catholics found a significant entry point in 1823 when Peter Robinson was sent to Ireland to recruit poverty-stricken families. The Robinson settlement was north and east of Perth, but it added a new dimension to a largely Protestant settlement. The unprecedented labour force required to build the Rideau Canal between 1826 and 1832 also attracted large numbers of Irish Catholics seeking cash wages. The building of the canal also attracted French Canadians, already familiar with the task of carving farms from the edges of the forest. Beckwith Street by the canal was once known in Perth as the French settlement. The great famine migration of the 1840s would also see many Irish seek homes in the region, especially since their introduction to Upper Canada was more than likely the Rideau Canal itself.[61]

Roads

The Perth military settlement was imposed on the landscape. While it was intended to create and sustain an inland population near a canal route that could link east and west during war, the townsite was several miles from the obvious waterway. Though sited on a fertile clay plain, it was bordered on the north and south by bog swamp. Perth was better located to hide from an enemy than to play a strategic role in internal communication if the St. Lawrence frontier were threatened.

Access by road to Perth in its pioneer stages, and indeed throughout the first half of the nineteenth century, was atrocious. Settlement in Upper Canada usually followed accessible riverine and lakeshore lands. Imposing a pattern of occupation on a landscape such as the Rideau military settlements took courage, if not arrogance. Getting access to one's land, let alone clearing it, became a settler's nightmare. Before technological improvements could force a road to run as straight as a surveyor's chain-link, it was human and beast against the elements. Pioneers waited expectantly for snow and ice to facilitate travel!

Rev. George Jehoshaphat Mountain, accompanying his father, Jacob, the first Anglican bishop of Quebec, to Perth in 1820, described the Brockville road as consisting of roots, rocks, sticks, stumps, holes, and bogs:

> The holes, however, and the sloughs are of course much worse in the wet season, and the travellers have sometimes been obliged to leave waggon and horses sticking fast till they could procure a yoke of oxen to pull them out. An Irishman in the service of Major Powell of Perth, being asked by his master how he had got along upon the road (with a waggon), replied, that he had got along pretty well, for he had found bottom in every place but one.[62]

The early settlements in Kitley and Bastard townships opened roads to the St. Lawrence River well before the founding of Perth. The first key roads to Perth came from Brockville via Toledo and from Gananoque via Delta and Portland, both needing to cross the Rideau system. Oliver's Ferry (now Rideau Ferry), in existence since 1816, was the landing area for travellers heading north to Perth (Lanark #1). While the first settlers arrived via Portland, the Brockville link via the ferry became the most important. Bytown was accessible by 1818 via the early Richmond or Franktown Road, which entered Perth on the 2nd line of Drummond, or North Street (Lanark #10). The old Kingston Road snaked south along the Leeds side of the Rideau Lakes to Portland, a route largely abandoned after the building of Highway #15. The Perth Road to Kingston went beyond the Scotch Line via Westport and was built as a plank road in 1852; John A. Macdonald had sponsored the road since 1844 to give Kingston greater access to its northern hinterland. A private road company developed an improved route to Smiths Falls in the 1850s (Highway #43), and the Lanark Road (secondary highway #511) was an important northern link from the beginning of the Lanark military settlement.[63]

Other roads fanned out from Perth southwest to Christie Lake and west to McDonalds Corners and north to Mississippi Lake. Some were toll routes. A sense of the old network can be experienced by taking the "old Perth Road" to Ferguson's Falls. In the 1880s, stage-coaches ran daily to the village of Lanark and to Glen Tay; twice weekly to Maberly and Westport; and three times a week to Ferguson's Falls.[64] The pioneer routes reflect the forced centrality of Perth within the original pattern of settlement; they helped sustain Perth's service role and have become etched and engraved into the landscape. Highway #7 from Toronto to Ottawa (built in 1931-32) is the only route not following a pioneer path out of Perth, as it bisects an old pattern of township roads.

Canals

The Tay and Rideau rivers were the natural routes to the wider world. The wild rivers were used with "difficulty and loss of property," according to Rev. Bell, but everyone anticipated canalization. In August 1824, Perth merchant and assemblyman William Morris presided over a public meeting to promote the Tay and Rideau canals. On the 27th of January 1826, "thirty-seven gentlemen, consisting of ministers, magistrates and half-pay officers sat down to a good dinner and to drink wine to show their approbation of his exertions."[65] Morris confirmed that the Rideau Canal would be constructed and that legislation would include powers to improve the navigation of the Tay.

Building the Rideau Canal between 1826 and 1832 affected the fortunes of Perth. It was one of the largest capital projects ever undertaken by the Imperial government in British North America. On the insistence of Lieut.-Col. John By, Royal Engineers, the military canal was given a commercial bearing by the construction of steamboat locks which would better serve the frontier. The intense schedule involved work being let by contract at 22 lock and dam sites stretched over 125 miles. It required a large and mobile labour force that had to be fed and supplied. Settlers and merchants around Perth found ample employment in hauling materials and delivering goods. The network of roads cut to construction sites greatly increased the amount of roadway along the corridor. The Rideau Canal imposed an east-west orientation between Ottawa and Kingston; formerly, Brockville, on the St. Lawrence, had been the outlet. When the canal opened in 1832, it became the main route for bulk transportation and passenger movement in Upper Canada; in 1847, completion of the St. Lawrence canals largely restricted the Rideau to regional trade.

While the building of this corridor encouraged growth in the town, serious doubts emerged over the future of the Tay. When the Weatherhead family of future Port Elmsley erected a mill dam on the Tay in 1829, Perth residents were shocked to realize that they might lose their avenue to the Rideau. With the Rideau Canal receiving government priority and the town's elite perceiving a

William Morris (1786-1858), Perth's most influential citizen of the first half of the 19th century and founder of the Tay Navigation Company. Born in Paisley, Scotland, he settled in Perth in 1816 where he became a general merchant and militia colonel. Elected to the House of Assembly in 1820 he served 16 years, before being appointed to the Legislative Council of Upper Canada in 1836 and to the new Legislative Council of the United Provinces in 1841. He was auditor-general 1844-46, and president of the Executive Council 1846-48. He was Chairman of the Board of Trustees at the creation of Queen's University in 1841. (Courtesy Queen's University Archives, William Morris Papers)

blockage of the river, they decided to take things into their own hands.

On the 30th of November 1830, William Morris called a town meeting to raise money for a private canal. With considerable perseverance, Morris pushed through the legislature a bill to create the Tay Navigation Company on 16 March 1831. The first slate of officers consisted of an interchangeable group of conservative magistrates, merchants, and half-pay officers, including Morris as president, and George Buchanan, Alexander Fraser, Henry Graham, John McKay, Alexander McMillan, Roderick Matheson, and George Hume Reade.[66]

Anticipating the Rideau Canal's bringing economic growth and concerned about being left behind, the clique embarked on a naive, if well-intentioned attempt to build the first Tay Canal. The company's officers ran into opposition not over the intention to build a canal but over the means by which it was undertaken. The Tay Navigation Co. used its influence to obtain Cockburn's Island in the middle of the river, set aside by the government for public purposes and markets (the Town Hall was built on one of the lots not severed). It split the community over its sale of island lots to finance the canal, and other political disputes arose over the management of canal construction, funding, and tolls. Canal controversies often pitted Conservatives against Reformers.

The first Tay Canal was built using funds from the sales of company shares, the sale of Cockburn Island lots, and loans from government and the Bank of Upper Canada, and with donations from two merchant houses in Montreal. The Royal Engineers on the Rideau Canal also provided some materials. Morris bitterly complained about people in Perth who "have never to this hour afforded the slightest assistance to a company which by perseverence in the face of almost insurmountable difficulties have enhanced the value of property at Perth to an incredible amount."[67]

The legacy of the Tay Navigation Co. was a debt-ridden, shallow, inadequate trough where the hopes of Perth were gradually drowned. Costly delays and alterations saw the canal open two years late, in 1834. Five cheaply constructed rubble masonry or timber locks only 90ft. by 20ft. (the Rideau Canal Locks were 134' by 33') with a draught no deeper than three and a half feet, restricted access. The original dams and swing bridges have disappeared, but a discerning eye can still trace a couple of lock sites (there were three locks in Port Elmsley) and a miserable little channel at one bend in the river. Most embarrassing for the company, a Perth-built steamer, the *Enterprise*, was unable to navigate the route; costly transshipment of goods between Rideau steamers and Tay barges at Stonehouse Island (Perth Landing) and Port Elmsley was the alternative. Several barges were built that could navigate by sail or be towed from Perth to Montreal.

Tow path along Tay River and Canal below Perth, c. 1900. The canal was provided with a tow path as far as the old lock site of Dowsen's just before the great marsh. The interrupted tow path was symbolic of the canal, too weedy and shallow for most Rideau Canal steamers, and limited in scope and purpose. (Postcard, collection of author)

Limitations on navigation, however, encouraged a vicious circle, wherein in-adequate tolls on the inefficient system led to insufficient maintenance, so that by the 1850s the canal's timber slides were the chief source of income for the beleaguered company. The first Tay Canal was built simply to raise the revenues that would enable future improvements. The Rideau Canal, in contrast, had been built, using public funds, to the highest standards (in debt as well as engineering), partly to avoid costly and frequent renewal.[68]

The failure of the Tay Canal by the late 1840s did not prevent lumbermen from taking advantage of the system to drive their square timber and sawlogs to Quebec. There was diversity to Perth's timber supply, including stands of oak, elm, hemlock, and cedar, as well as the dominant pine. However, the Tay water-shed was limited in its resource base. Furthermore, distant lands were better served on their own waterways, such as the Mississippi River to the north, which significantly hemmed in Perth's hinterland. Nor did the Tay have the volume of water that would drive a water-based industrial complex like that on the Missis-sippi. Perth had big aspirations on too small a pond.

Completion of the St. Lawrence River canals by 1847 siphoned much of the westward movement of trade and immigrants that used to pass through the Rideau corridor. The growth of Canada West in the 1850s and early 1860s, encouraged by the Crimean War, reciprocity with the United States, and then the American Civil War, and the increasing maturity of the outlying districts, helped create a building boom in Perth. However, the town's horizon was shrinking. Its adminis-trative responsibilities, which once included Bytown (now Ottawa), decreased with boundary changes. While Perth-area farmers and artisans helped supply the broad Ottawa Valley lumber trade with pork, oatmeal and flour, tools, wagons, and men, the actual frontier was moving beyond Perth's reach and creating empires based in Ottawa, Arnprior, Renfrew, and Pembroke, rather than inland Perth.

Because of the difficulty of crossing the Tay, Perth's main business district had been slow to develop. Building of the Rideau Canal sparked a construction boom in Perth and contributed at least a generation of Scots and Irish stonemasons who settled in the area after its completion. Setting the style for the commercial district was the Matheson complex at Gore and Foster streets. It is remarkable, when one considers that the stone buildings at this, Perth's main intersection, all date from the 1840s, that all are still standing and none occupied by a bank. These classically styled Georgian commercial buildings – Shaws, the Hicks Ho-tel, Meighen Block, and James Brothers initially fronted onto Foster Street, the town's main commercial street until mid-century.

Many of Gore Street's stone buildings were erected between 1830 and 1850 during favourable economic conditions. The mercantile buildings are domestic in scale, usually no more than two storeys high, and celebrate Georgian symmetry, as in the Erwin Block, 1832. The ghost sign, painted on the stone, at the main entrance, proclaiming the offices of Thomas M. Radenhurst Attorney at Law, hint at its legacy. Across the street, equally impressive in their simplicity, are the Brookes Block and its neighbour, the Mathews Building, which form part of a wonderful stone row including the Sheriffs House, the Thomas Building, and Harry's Cafe.

Buildings can tell a lot about who lived in them, why they were built, and for what purpose. Roderick Matheson (1793-1873) put up an imposing and dignified complex of residence, mercantile outlet, and warehousing, all set within walled gardens. The complex reflects an era of prosperity following construction of the Rideau Canal. The Matheson House is a national historic site and home to the Perth Museum. As a half-pay and militia officer, Matheson had the seniority and prestige to build a little fortress close to the important road leading out of town. As a general merchant and politician, he had the resources and stature to erect a prominent building on a main street.

Severely plain in design, the five-bay, two-storey house, with finely crafted stonework, is clearly of Georgian influence. Set within walled gardens on either side, the house is a model of symmetry, focusing on the three central bays, which project forward, supporting a classical pediment with bull's-eye window. The house is smaller and simpler than the type that recalled American designs and English mid-Georgian models. Matheson and the builder may have had to take into account some local factors: the more compact the building, the easier it was to heat. Also, the widespread shortage of servants willing or able to work in a household made a smaller dwelling convenient. Rev. William Bell insinuated that relations between the master of the house and what servants he could hire were too compact and warm.

Canals and Immigration

The Rideau Canal linked the ocean ports of the St. Lawrence with the Great Lakes, and it became a major conduit for immigrants entering Upper Canada and the United States between 1832 and 1847. Approximately 30,000 immigrants in 1843 used the Ottawa-Rideau system; numbers peaked at 89,562 in 1847.[69] Immigrants were towed in crowded open barges by steamers from Montreal via the Rideau Canal to Kingston, where they would transfer to other vessels heading further west. Many families disembarked for Perth as their planned destination. However, enticements along the new canal were more than enough to lure some individuals and families to seek land in the vicinity. By 1834 Perth had its own Tay Canal branch to the wider system.

Continued chain migration influenced many British immigrants to settle in the Perth area. When the North Quarter Glasgow Emigration Society sought subscriptions to support its cause in 1841, it invoked people's prior knowledge of the Rideau area, claiming "They have many friends in Upper Canada comfortably situated."[70] In the absence of state aid, immigrants from Great Britain came out in various colonization schemes and societies or on their own.

Immigration to Perth and area had been influenced by its inland location, early military dominance, and British population. Although much has been written about the Scottish character in the origins of Perth, by 1842, the largest foreign-born element in Lanark County was Irish. In the 1871 census, the population claiming Irish origins made up half of Perth. The population by origin was Irish, 1,213; Scottish, 695; English, 359; French, 71; Welsh, 23; and 14 others.[71]

In 1846 Perth had 7 churches, 7 taverns, 5 lawyers, 3 physicians, a bank agency (City Bank of Montreal), and a printer and weekly newspaper to service the needs of a population of 1,800 as well as the outlying area. Perth also had 15 shoemakers, 12 tailors, 11 stores, 7 coopers and blacksmiths, 4 tanneries and wagon makers, 3 weavers, tinsmiths, foundries, distilleries, 2 breweries, druggists and watchmakers; a cabinet maker, a sawmill, and a grist mill. A stage-coach ran three days a week to Brockville.[72]

When the St. Lawrence Canals were completed in 1847, the Rideau Canal ceased to be the most important east-west link, and later migrants would be oblivious to the attractions of Perth and district. By mid-century, Perth ceased to be as attractive a destination. Land not taken up in the vicinity was probably too marginal for effective agricultural pursuit; the Rideau Canal had lost its competitive edge; boundary alterations had reduced Perth from a district to a mere county seat; and Ottawa was emerging as the dominant centre for the region.

CHAPTER FOUR

Everyday Life in Early Perth

Education

When Perth was founded, religion and education were not separate fields of endeavour. Ministers of the church were among the lucky few who had received higher education, and they saw it as their duty to promote and advance teaching and education. Presbyterianism in particular championed education as a means to success and salvation. The Scottish population in Perth was well served by several leaders in education and religion. Against the entrenched elite in Toronto – "the Family Compact" – and the power of Bishop John Strachan and his attempt to establish the Anglican faith in the colony, men such as William Bell, Malcolm Cameron, and William Morris played important roles in striving for the equal rights of Scots.

From the origins of Upper Canada in 1791, clergy reserves, amounting to one-seventh of each surveyed township, had been set aside for the support of the Protestant clergy. The government at York defined the Protestant clergy as the established Church of England, with all others falling into different categories of "dissenters." Rev. William Bell had to abandon a successful school which he had begun in 1817, when the Anglican Rev. Michael Harris arrived in Perth in 1819. The fight over clergy reserves and access to and support of education became the first political controversy of the settlement.

Malcolm Cameron, as founder of the Bathurst, later Perth *Courier* in 1834, was at first a moderate Reformer and later a radical "Clear Grit," who fought in the assembly for dissolution of the clergy reserves. He believed that state support should be removed from all religions or apportioned equally to all that had a regularly constituted ministry. William Morris, Perth's first representative to the assembly (1820-36), before being appointed to the legislative council, led the conservative forces in Perth, which thought that the Church of Scotland deserved equal funding from the reserves in recognition of its national status in the homeland. Needless to say, the Anglican hierarchy could not sustain its hold on exclusive support.

When King's College was founded by royal charter in 1827, it was to be Anglican and funded in part from a quarter-million acres of crown reserves. William Morris fought and cajoled for a separate Presbyterian college. He, more than any other individual, was responsible for a royal charter being granted for Queen's College in Kingston in 1841. Bell, Cameron, and Morris helped secure a more balanced religious and educational structure for Perth and the rest of the province. However, if these three Scots met at the corner of Foster and Gore, there would have been heated debate and recrimination. Typical of the divisions in Scots society, Morris had led the "Auld Kirk" out of Bell's church, Bell had been an enemy of Cameron's, and Morris and Cameron were on opposite sides of the political spectrum.[73]

With the passing of the District School Act of 1819, and Perth's new role as district town in 1823, a district or grammar school in which mathematics and the

Sampler embroidered in 1854 by Elizabeth James Hicks (1839-1918), then aged 15, using patterns from a tutor or teacher. The symbols are typical of at least three other Perth-area samplers, including the large Georgian stone house with familiar fan-light doorway. Samplers were designed by girls as part of a routine in the teaching of domestic abilities. (Collection of author)

classics were taught was opened, in addition to a common school. In 1823 John Stewart (1788-1881), educated at Trinity College, Dublin, and founder of Perth's first newspaper, the *Independent Examiner*, was appointed teacher at the grammar school.[74] An old stone school-house stood on the southeast side of D'Arcy between Gore and Wilson streets from 1834 to 1846.

Some of Perth's social elite would never be comfortable with a common school, so several small private schools (some were called dame schools) were run in town up to the late 1830s. Benjamin Tett, later a lumberman, forwarder, and miller based at Bedford Mills on the Rideau, taught from 1823 to 1825 at a small semi-private school. His successor, John Wilson, a legal student, later assisted at the grammar school. (It was over the honour of Miss Hughes, another private school teacher, that John Wilson killed Robert Lyon, in Perth's last fatal duel in 1833.) Robert Lees, later a prominent politician and Ottawa lawyer, ran a school on D'Arcy Street, and Roderick Matheson sponsored several teachers, who in the process of teaching his children took on other students. Some of the best-known teachers were the three Misses Jessop, who ran a school on Brock Street; they were replaced by their sister-in-law, Mrs. Jessop, who insisted that her students give confessions every Friday for their misdemeanours during the week. Male private-school teachers included Dawson Kerr, and Messrs. Hudson and Tully. After the passing of the School Act of 1841, private schools waned, although a Mrs. Corbett and two sister combinations, Fraser and Sinclair, kept boarding and day schools for young women into the 1840s.[75]

Religion

Religion had a remarkable impact on the social, cultural, and educational life of Upper Canada and Ontario. In the nineteenth century, it formed a structure of order, familiarity, and a sense of tradition and place in a developing community. Perth played a prominent role in the regional development of churches in eastern Ontario, and several residents became known for their contributions to religion and education in Canada. Although none of Perth's original church structures survives, distinctive replacements form a Victorian legacy.

Perth went through two eras in church development. From 1816, churches were in their pioneering phase, with ministers travelling to see their adherents in the surrounding countryside as well as trying to maintain simple places of worship in town. As churches became more organized, and parishes or circuits shrank to more manageable size, a new stability was reflected in the erection, particularly, in the Victorian era, of symbolic places of worship. St. John's Roman Catholic and St. James Anglican, with their tall spires, still inspire Perth's skyline.

The earliest ministers and priests in Perth were missionaries. The first mission-

ary was the Rev. William Bell of Edinburgh, who took his calling in 1817 to develop First Presbyterian Church. His surviving diaries, papers, and reminiscences
are the richest source of information on Perth and district. Casting aspersions on
non-Calvinists, Bell roamed widely through early Rideau settlements spreading
the word of God. He always gave graphic descriptions of his arduous travel. On one
such occasion, in July 1827, he sought a path through a rugged swamp:

> We were told however it might be passed at a particular place; but after making
> the attempt and getting both ourselves and horses rolled in mud, to say nothing
> of the danger of losing them altogether, for it was as bad as any peat bog, we were
> forced to turn back and leave them at the next farm house. We then proceeded
> on foot, and got through, by the assistance of logs and bushes, the best we could.
> The heat was excessive, and the mosquitos, which were always more numerous in
> swamps than any where else, annoyed us dreadfully. At 10, A.M. we reached Mr.
> Buchanan's, where we met a kind reception. At 12, I preached in the barn to
> about 150 people.[76]

Father Pierre Jacques de La Mothe, a native of Gascony and a former chap-
lain of the de Watteville regiment, was the first Roman Catholic priest in Perth.
When Father John McDonnell (sometimes McDonald) was transferred from
Glengarry to Perth in 1823, he had to serve 3,640 parishioners in fourteen neigh-
bouring townships north of the Rideau. He was one of only seven priests then
serving in Upper Canada. The rapid expansion of the Irish labour force and of
French Canadians in the square timber trade and in construction of the Rideau
Canal added considerable numbers.[77]

When Rev. Michael Harris arrived in Perth in 1819, he was one of only thir-
teen Anglican ministers in Upper Canada. His responsibilities for the Church of
England included local townships as well as Lanark, Richmond, Beckwith, and
March. By 1832, four of the eight clergymen receiving government salaries in
the District of Bathurst were from Perth, including Bell and Harris (£100 each),
McDonald (£54), and a new Church of Scotland minister, Thomas Wilson
(£62.10s).[78]

Rev. John Griggs Peale started a Methodist chapel by 1821, but owing to the
vigorous presence of other clergymen, the traditional circuit-riding format of
Methodists did not have the same impact as elsewhere in the province. George
F. Playter, a minister in Perth in 1837, claimed in his *History of Methodism in
Canada* that "the people of these settlements were not favourable to Methodist
preachers, preferring the Presbyterian and Episcopal ministers; and Methodism
never made such progress in the frontier townships."[79] Its early strength in eastern Ontario lay in the older townships along the St. Lawrence and Lake Ontario.

Early churches were beset with financial problems and dispersed flocks. Owing to the lack of clergymen, ministers in many parishes were from the United Kingdom and their presence helped to maintain old traditions through cultural transfer. People of different denominations would attend a gathering simply to be part of a service. Different churches supported each other in fund raising for buildings or bells. Father John McDonnell, a Highlander, would thank Protestant contributors to a project by announcing their names in a service, usually followed by the comment, "Vera guid indeed for a heretic." When it came time for him to help build a new Presbyterian church, he got around canonical rules by helping to tear down the old one.[80] None of the pioneer churches of Perth is still in existence, but the building where Bell and Harris first preached in the "upper room," or officer's mess, at the old Red Inn, or Adamson House, still stands at 53-55 Craig Street.

While Calvinism was central to the Presbyterian outlook, it influenced several other denominations as well. Its theology included the concept of the Bible as the Word of God, the source of all true knowledge, and the idea that the actions of humans are determined from moment to moment by the mysterious and all-powerful providence of God. According to the doctrines of predestination and election, people, known only to God, received salvation and forgiveness for sins. In the process of believing and being sanctified, believers could participate and, by improving themselves through education, moral deeds, and even success in business, could prove or obtain salvation. Through such beliefs, all of society could be reformed, and faith would penetrate every aspect of social, political, and economic life. Such views affected spritual, social, and economic life in Perth.[81]

Upper Canada's temperance movement pulled together the concerns of all churches to oppose pioneer drunkenness, even if eastern Ontario temperance lodges tended to be organized by middle-class, well-established, American-origin people in the 1830s, as a kind of political buffer to the hard-drinking, ultra-loyal Irish Protestant immigrants forming Orange Lodges.[82] Orangeism was particularly strident and offered Irish Anglicans a means of retaining ethnic and cultural ties as well as religious and political clout. The battles between the "wets" and the "drys" carried on into the twentieth century and split more than ethnic groups and communities. Drinking split families as well.

Rev. William Bell, originally a light drinker, became an ardent promoter of total abstinence as the result of the intemperance of his son, William, Jr. Business instability and family tragedy in 1837 cast William, Jr., into an ever deeper pit of alcoholism, until he died from his affliction in 1844.[83] His father badgered the undutiful, ungrateful son and tried to impose a family-wide pledge of total abstinence in 1842. His daughter, Isabella Malloch, received the following command: "Know all men by this declaration that I, William Bell ... perceiving the awful and ruinous consequences which follow the use of intoxicating drinks, to the bodies and souls of mankind have resolved never again to use any of them myself, as a common beverage, nor to offer them to others; and to enjoin the same thing upon all my children, and their descendants ... in order that they be honest, industrious and temperate...."[84]

Her father's declaration ignited Isabella's perception of her liberty of conscience, and she scolded him, saying that he was not justified in calling down the vengeance of heaven on her family. The debate was indicative of the polarization over such issues as liquor distribution, especially in a town like Perth, where powerful religious influences came up against strong interests sustaining Perth's distilling industry.[85]

Social Activities

There are few references to social or cultural activities in pioneer society other than religious, military, or political events. Home and family life was central to social organization, but most descriptions ignore the details of everyday life, as compared to social interaction with friends and community. Elections, militia days, agricultural fairs, church functions, and temperance gatherings would pull at least a part of the community together. Depictions of tavern life, dances, singing, games, and home entertainment are rare. As Brockville-area immigrant Thomas Graham complained in 1827 to his mother in Wexford, Ireland: "The chief objection folks have to this country, is the want of pleasures, but these are vanities."[86]

The diary of Rev. William Bell vividly portrayed the social activities which the Calvinist missionary resented. Surprising, he showed little resistance to dancing on winter nights, when "young people made parties, at private houses, to enjoy this amusement." He described with some disgust, even though he was frequently a guest, partying by the half-pay officers and elite:

> Most of our gentry in the village and neighbourhood formerly in the Army were fond of splendid entertainment. In this way they often indulged far beyond their means and were generally in debt. The civilians fired by the ambitions of their military neighbours gave their parties too, and all thought that every winter a ball must be given. Then there were several public subscription balls on the evening of St George's, St Andrew's, St. Patrick's Day. But at length the progress of the party spirit rendered these assemblies few and far between after 1830. At one party given by Thomas Radenhurst, a young lawyer, to which I and my family were invited, I observed an expense which must long have been felt by a young man. To see ... the Rev. Mr. Harris, an honest Hibernian Episcopal clergyman ... of his age and dimensions, for he was neither young nor slender, cutting his capers in the gayest company, afforded amusement even among those who cared nothing for religion.[87]

Elections were another excuse for public festivities. Bell described Perth's first election, in July 1820, when William Morris defeated Benjamin DeLisle. For almost a week, polls were open in Perth, and on the final day a victor was crowned: "Mr. Morris was declared duly elected. The crowd then proceeded to chair the successful candidate. The procession paraded the streets, several hours, huzzaing and singing patriotic songs, while the inhabitants as they passed, regaled them with wine, sprits etc. The evening was spent in merriment and various kinds of amusements...."[88]

Local agricultural societies encouraged better methods of farming and marketing, and they helped focus interest in fairs and friendly competition. Fair days had existed from the beginning of settlement, and the annual Perth (and Dis-

The Rival Candidates William Morris Esqr and Alex Thom Esqr On the Hustings. Perth. Upper Canada. Wednesday Twentyeighth July 1828

"On the stumps," in 1828. William Morris (1786-1858), MLA since 1820 and a general merchant, defeated Alexander Thom (1775-1845), pensioned officer and former military surgeon who built the first mills in Perth. The fervent mix of old politics, new issues, and competing religious and ethnic groups made for a colourful political stage. Elections lasted several days until a winner was declared. (An original by F.H. Consitt dated 1830, in Perth Museum)

trict) Agricultural Society Fair emerged from a series of events that used to be held at market square, on the site of the Town Hall. It shifted to Greenlee's Corners in 1874 and to Fairholm Park (behind the Perth planing mill) from 1891 to 1912, until it reached its present site. Fair days continue to reinforce Perth's traditional role as a service centre to a wide agricultural hinterland.[89]

A form of public entertainment frequently referred to by Rev. Bell as the "charivari" was being actively suppressed in 1846. It involved a parade of partygoers intent on disrupting the first night of a married couple, especially if the marriage involved a widow or widower. Bell described a Perth charivari in 1845:

> They are of French origin and are often practiced in the Lower Province; only in the case of widows or widowers marrying. Horns, bells, kettles, or anything that will make noise soon collect a mob. A coffin is carried to the door, containing one of the party, dressed as to represent the ghost of the deceased wife or husband. The coffin is opened, the ghost walks into the house, and makes certain demands of money, which must be complied with, or mischief follows. The attendants meanwhile, in all kinds of fantastic dresses and masks, or having their faces painted, are singing, dancing, making speeches or cracking jokes. Sometimes these rude intrusions are resisted and serious consequences follow.[90]

Late in 1844, Bell described William Spalding and Isabella Smith hoping to avoid the embarrassing spectacle, even though the former's wife had died only seven months earlier: "They expected to slip home in the dark quietly avoiding a charivari. But in this they were mistaken. It soon got wind, and horns, bells, and old pans were soon heard all over the town, making music anything but harmonious. After the party had assembled at Mr. Spalding's house, about a mile from Perth, he was glad to give them something to eat and drink, and three dollars besides, to get quit of them."[91] Bell may have raised the charivari himself because he was not paid for performing the wedding ceremony.

CHAPTER FIVE

Victorian County Seat

Defining a Role

In 1850 the former boundaries of Bathurst District were abolished under the United Province's new municipal system which was based on counties and townships. Perth lost a considerable amount of its public jurisdiction with the separation of Carleton County, including Bytown (Ottawa), in 1850, and the separation of Renfrew County in 1861. With its jurisdiction confined to Lanark County, Perth's influence was severely diminished. However, Perth was incorporated as a village on 27 September 1850 (effective 1851), and it was allowed to expand its townsite into three distinct wards: East, Centre, and West. Perth originally consisted of lots 2 and 3 in the 1st Concession of Drummond Township. The extension included lots 1 in the 1st concession and lots 2 and 3 in the 2nd, allowing the town to absorb the park lots originally surveyed but not included in the townsite, as well as Carolina Village, west of Wilson Street and north of the Tay. Perth was incorporated as a town on 9 September 1853 (effective 1854), and its population was approximately 2,000. A handsome new town hall erected in 1863 proclaimed Perth's presence, but its future was less certain.[92]

A building boom in the 1850s and early 1860s created many of the stone commercial buildings on Gore Street. The shrinking horizon of Perth's influence was countered in part by the increasing wealth being made from the land near the town. The old group of half-pay officers able to invest in local business gave way to a new commercial elite, which included miller John Haggart, manufacturer

Alexander Kippen, machinist William Lillie, contractor Hugh Ryan, and merchants John Doran, James Allan, Thomas Brooke, Arthur Meighen, J. T. Henderson, and James and William Mair. However, Perth had sluggish growth between 1860 and 1880. Official estimates show that Perth grew from 2,465 to 2,467 in those two decades. The population rose in the early 1860s and fell with the depression in the late 1860s and the 1870s.

The railway reached Perth in 1859, but it did not have the expected impact. It was only a branch of a line – the Brockville and Ottawa (B&O) – that better served Smiths Falls and Carleton Place. It was once thought that the arrival of the branch line of the B & O in 1859 buried the first Tay Canal. The canal was dormant long before, however, and the railway offered minimal help to Perth. Not unlike the canal, Perth's first railway was a cul-de-sac. The first train, a wood-burning locomotive hauling two coaches from Smiths Falls, coughed and choked into Perth on the 17th of February, 1859, having taken nine hours and

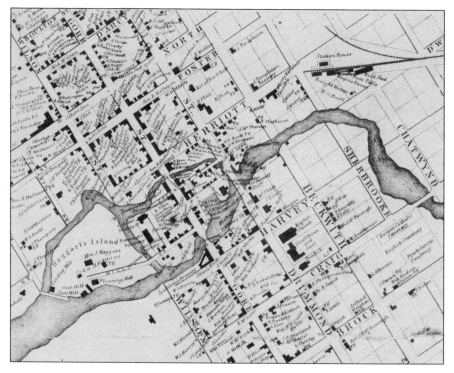

In 1863, Perth was shifting westward into the park lots above North Street (acquired from Drummond Township in 1851), and the central business district was clustering along Gore and Foster streets. Detail from Map of the Counties of Lanark and Renfrew, Canada West, by H. F. Walling (Prescott, D. F. Putnam, 1863). (NA, NMC 21,920)

Perth Town Hall built between 1863 and 1864, with its second storey public hall, expressed confidence in its classically conservative design. The clock tower is one of Perth's landmarks. (Photo c. 1900, courtesy John J. Stewart)

forty-five minutes to cover the distance. Even the horses were laughing. Eventually the railway was programmed to leave three times daily (except Sunday) to Smiths Falls, whence a connection would deliver passengers to Brockville – a seven-and a-half-hour trip. It was about half a day's trip to Montreal. On 23 August 1872, even the Perth *Courier* admitted that the railway had "not accomplished all that was anticipated" and the "great increase of population promised ... never happened." While it was an opening to the outside, it did not inspire commerce, although farmers and lumbermen found it convenient to ship produce, livestock and resources. Pat Donegan, the first engineer on the Perth branch of the B & O, was its last, 25 years later.[93]

In the 1870s the *Courier* was concerned that unless the community provided bonuses to railway development, it would leave Perth "a forlorn, decaying town, forever shut off from direct railway communication from East, West, North and South." In 1878, the Montreal *Commercial Review* described Perth as the first important town west of the capital.[94] Belden's *Illustrated Atlas of Lanark and*

Renfrew Counties commented in 1881 that "Perth cannot by any means be classed under the head of a manufacturing town."[95] Perhaps cognizant of Perth's motto, "Make Haste Slowly" (festina lente sed certo), writers for the atlas pointed out: "To one more acquainted with the activity and push of western life, the place on first sight looks 'slow', but a closer acquaintance will invariably confirm ... its prosperity and generally satisfactory condition."[96]

Expectations of mineral resources had always fascinated townsfolk, especially with enticing bits of evidence gathered up by Dr. James Wilson, an amateur geologist and local physician in Perth for 48 years. In the 1870s a developing mining sector was seen as a real possibility. Visions of a planned blast furnace and developments already under way for a limited but forever hopeful mining industry based on local deposits of apatite, mica, feldspar, graphite, and iron ore led to speculation. The iron deposits never materialized, but phosphate derived from apatite and used in fertilizer produced some small-scale shallow mines in North Burgess Township in the 1870s and 1880s, followed by mining of mica in the same deposits around the turn of the century. Graphite was mined near Rideau Ferry, and the Timmins family, later famous in northern Ontario, had interests in local feldspar. The old bolt factory on the Tay River once housed dozens of young girls who thumb-trimmed sheets and blocks of mica for market.[97]

Sheep being herded to market on Gore Street, c. 1890s. Market days reminded the town of Perth's close interconnection with the rural community. (Courtesy John J. Stewart)

The agricultural sector was also undergoing a major transition in the latter portion of the nineteenth century. Perth was the rural centre for a large country market, but it had lost its dominance to several other regional centres since the pioneer days when Bytown and Perth were the market towns in the Bathurst District. Mixed farming had become the norm, with a combination of cash crops, dairying, and livestock. Locally, oats and barley were major cash crops, with some of the demand coming from Perth's two distilleries (at their peak between the 1870s and 1916) and the processing of oats at Haggart's mill.

Driven by the commercial market, introduction of the Holstein cow, availability of grazing lands, and new technologies for the safe and efficient transport of dairy products, cheese factories began dotting the landscape by the 1870s. Perth saw production of the world's biggest cheese in September 1892 at the Dominion Experimental Dairy Station; the 22,000 pound mammoth cheese was put on display at the World's Columbian Exposition in Chicago in 1893. Legends still exist about the making, transport, display, and final dispersion of the big cheese, which attracted crowds of spectators as it made its way to Chicago on a specially built flat car designed by Matthew Stanley. At the fair it drew huge crowds and its weight demolished the original display platform. Sir Thomas Lipton, the British tea magnate, purchased the mass; a few scraps are on display at the Perth Museum.[98] Dairy production soared late in the century: of 1,123 cheese factories in the province in 1899, 75 percent were in eastern Ontario. By 1922, the Perth Cheese Board was made up of 18 co-operating factories in Lanark County.

The solid masonry buildings of Perth's old merchants dominate Gore Street while Victorian fancy reigns on Drummond Street north of the Tay River. Along this canopied promenade at one time were some of Perth's choicest addresses. Stately Second Empire residences set within lavishly planted yards provided a backdrop to the character-defining street trees. It is interesting how the loss of one feature devalues the whole. The street is virtually intact, but when one compares the present image, lacking a uniform planting of sugar maple, with historic photographs of this street, the loss is significant.

The CPR and the Second Tay Canal

If Perth had a golden age, it came in the 1880s, when transient workers almost doubled the population. A key trigger was transportation development and construction of railways and a canal. There was a new spirit in Perth with the anticipation of growth around railways, resources, manufacturing, and Sir John A. Macdonald's National Policy. The town swelled with workers and expectations.

In 1882, the *Expositor* exclaimed that Perth would soon "have all the essen-

Looking west on Drummond Street from the tower of St. James Anglican Church, c. 1890. The new middle classes built roomy Victorian houses on the park lots above North Street. In the foreground, with carriage sheds, is Summit House (1823). (Postcard, collection of author)

tials for growth into a large and prosperous town ... a city in about three years." Perth was experiencing a bona fide boom, with competing railway projects constructing parallel lines within the town boundaries at the same time. The Ontario and Quebec Railway would win the contest over the Toronto and Ottawa Railway (one can still detect the abandoned culverts and bridge foundation parallel to Highway #7 to Actinolite), but more than 1,000 men camped in and about Perth during construction in 1882. When it opened in 1884, the Ontario and Quebec Railway had became the Canadian Pacific Railway's (CPR) major trunk line between Montreal and Toronto and the branch line of the old B & O to Smiths Falls was absorbed into the CPR line.

The town granted a bonus and 25 acres of land to the CPR for erection of factory buildings, where passenger, freight, dining, kitchen, and sleeping cars, as well as flat and box cars, could be assembled. Until the fire of 1904, the CPR was Perth's major employer.[99] Although the Ontario line of the CPR was designed to link major metropolitan centres, the railway created opportunities for local producers. Both the Stanley and the Hicks carriage factories began producing wagons for the opening western markets. Perth also began to participate more fully in the textile trade with its expanding Code Mill. Incentives were flowing from the National Policy, the Macdonald government's attempt to foster the growth of Canadian manufacturing behind high tarriff barriers. The country experienced depressions on either side of this boom. Nevertheless, Perth's population grew to 3,136 by 1891 – reflecting its largest increase in any decade for which statistics are available.

While small carriage-making and furniture factories, tanneries and distilleries, shops, artisans, mills, and services characterized the early work world of Perth, the CPR was among the first industrial plants involving large numbers of wage employees. The homes of these workers were built beyond the town centre near the old French settlement on Beckwith Street, in Carolina Village, south and west of Wilson and Foster streets, and in clusters in the East Ward. Associated with this more distinct working-class community came the rise of early labour

The Hicks family at leisure in their home on North Street, 1898. Thomas Hicks Sr., carriage-maker, and son-in-law Richard McCarthy, hardware merchant, play crokinole, while other family members read or play. Electric light extended evening activities and encouraged reading and indoor games. Clockwise from left: Edith, Elizabeth, Anna, Thomas and Minnie Hicks, Elizabeth Hicks McCarthy, Etta, Richard and Harold McCarthy, Thomas and Bessie Dickinson. (Collection of author)

organizations searching for better working and economic conditions. The Knights of Labor reported 20 members in Perth in 1883, and 175 in 1888, before falling to 50 the next year. However, Perth was a small base on which to develop any kind of movement. Seasonal job fluctuations, minimal job protection, and workers transience allowed employers to displace individuals thought to be leaders of labour organizations.[100]

Despite fast railways, canals also experienced a boom in the 1880s which saw locks or canals built or rebuilt on the St. Lawrence, Welland, Trent, and Sault St. Marie and Murray Canals. Not to be smitten by the failure of the first watery cul-de-sac, town luminaries sought revival of the Tay Canal. Still considered a cheaper method to move bulk products or resources, the canal reappeared not in private hands, but in the public domain. Claiming that Perth deserved public funding, and that a canal was a priority to facilitate expected development around phosphate mining and iron smelting, Mayor Francis A. Hall and MP John Haggart promoted a new waterway. After a feasibilty study undertaken by the government, John Page, chief engineer of canals, commented that "it was unlikely that a new waterway could compete with existing transportation, especially in lieu of the commercial decline of the Rideau Canal." However, Haggart got some support from fellow Conservative MP Moss Kent Dickinson, a mill-owner from Manotick, who called for improvement of the Tay as a major feeder to the Rideau system after 45 industries experienced an interruption of water-power in 1881. Haggart had influence on Parliament Hill, and not unlike William Morris and the first canal, was at the head of a local Conservative elite.[101]

Haggart believed that a new canal would secure an iron smelter for Perth and several re-elections for himself; it would also benefit his own flour-milling business. The second Tay Canal was built in three stages, between 1882 and 1891, each extension putting Haggart and his ditch deeper into the public trough of public works expenditures.

Instead of following the twisted path of the original Tay Canal via Port Elmsley, the second canal used a cut about one mile long to Beveridges Bay on Lower Rideau Lake. Hopelessly over-budget and late, the canal section to Craig Street was completed in 1887 by contractors A. F. Manning and Angus P. Macdonald. The town of Perth celebrated its opening by holding a tribute to Macdonald at the Town Hall; his son had been killed in an explosion during construction.

Late in 1887, the town fathers decided that the canal would be useful to Perth only if it could be extended to the original basin, near the town centre. Just in time for the 1887 dominion election, the extension was approved, and Davis &

John Haggart Jr. (1836-1913) was Perth's most influential citizen of the second half of the 19th century and the man most responsible for building the second Tay Canal. Son of a mill owner, he spent a life in politics serving as Mayor of Perth and 41 years as a Member of Parliament for South Lanark. Haggart was a cabinet minister from 1888-1896, and as a leader of the Ontario Conservatives in Ottawa, was considered as a potential prime minister in 1894. While he was known for bagging party and government funds, he was alleged "to have an eye for plump and accessible lady typists," and was never elevated to the highest office. (NA, PA 26382)

Sons of Ottawa won the contract to revive the basin and build bridge supports at Craig, Beckwith, and Drummond streets. The swing bridges were let separately; the Beckwith span still survives. After this contract, Haggart attempted to arrange for unexpended sums to be put toward a further extension to his mill. A new bridge at Gore Street was built (the old stone bridge was demolished), and John O'Toole had excavated about as far as the swimming pond when Parliament got a whiff of Haggart's folly, and work was brought to an abrupt halt.[102]

During an exchange in the House of Commons between Sir Richard Cartwright and Sir John A. Macdonald in 1890, Cartwright commented on the Tay Canal: "This I understand, is a really useful work; it drains the County of Perth [Lanark]," to which the prime minister replied, "It drains the public treasury pretty well."

In 1891, an incredulous MP rose in debate concerning the cost of the canal:

> The whole result is that we have two little tugs, one little pleasure boat, two little rowboats, and one old scow navigating the Tay Canal. What a screaming farce that must be to the frisky Minister of Finance ... an expenditure of half a million resulting in a revenue of $58.81.... That canal, Mr. Speaker, will stand there for all time to come as it is now, a living monument of departmental imbecility if not something worse.... It was as gross a fraud perpetuated on the tax-payers of this country as was ever perpetuated by any government on any people.[103]

John Haggart was finally exposed in the House of Commons on 12 August 1891. He was accused of extending by unusual methods (one month before Haggart's fifth re-election), a canal known as "Haggart's Ditch" to Haggart's Is-

The Second Tay Canal built 1882-1892 as seen from Beckwith Street bridge, c. 1905. The canal offered a cheaper avenue for the export of bulk products, but from the commercial standpoint, it was completely unsuccesful. The canal and basin did contribute to the aesthetic enhancement of downtown Perth, in both the gardens planted by underworked bridgemasters and in the appeal of a placid body of water in the centre of town. (Postcard, collection of author)

land so that the steamer *John Haggart* could gain access to the wharves at Haggart's Mill. For this, Haggart was rewarded with the Railways and Canals portfolio in the federal cabinet in 1892.

The publicly built second canal was as much a commercial disappointment as the privately built first one. However, the opening of the second greatly enhanced Perth's position in the tourist and recreational industry then blossoming around the Rideau Lakes. With the operation of dual-purpose steamers as town boats out of Perth, and the rapid development of motor boating after 1901, the Tay became a link to this new seasonal market. Indeed, Rideau Ferry emerged as a recreational satellite community, where regattas held on civic holidays drew citizens to the lake.

The Tay Basin long criticized as an open sewer, became an object of beauty and admiration. The Perth bridgemaster, who swung the bridges open for larger boats, had so little to do that he took up gardening. Landscaping was encouraged by the Rideau Canal, but bridgmasters John Russell and Philip McParlan pushed it to new heights. For over half a century the basin was a gardener's delight, and the floral crest and emblem on the banks near the Gore Street bridge are a legacy from their efforts.[104]

Needless to say, after the Tay Canal experience, investors, public or private, were cautious about transportation schemes for Perth. In the 1890s William Clyde Caldwell of Lanark got nowhere trying to sell Perth on a proposed electric North Lanark Railway. No longer would transportation "fixes" speed up Perth's growth. In the twentieth century, automobiles invaded small towns, tearing at the fabric that held communities together but also bringing opportunities based on the networks that cars created and the mobility that they made possible. Highways have served to integrate Perth into the eastern Ontario mainstream, and their location has done little to damage the character of the town. In an inland settlement such as Perth, transportation has always been a central concern.

Outward Bound

Perth has seen many of its young move westward. The first exodus involved many original grantees in the military settlement who sought better land and matrimonial possibilities elsewhere. Even after completion of the Rideau Canal in 1832, Malcolm Cameron (1808-1876) began assembling land in western Upper Canada, including 4,000 acres of Indian reserve land as part of a syndicate

The *John Haggart* at the entrance to Beveridge Locks on the second Tay Canal, c. 1890s. The commercial limitations of the second Tay Canal were balanced by the growing interest in recreational boating on the Rideau Canal. Steamers like the *John Haggart* served a public excursion trade while skiffs and later motor-boats (by the 1900s) drew attention to the delights of private leisure boating. The Hicks family are seen in *Jumbo*, their first boat. (Collection of author)

and 6,500 acres of land near Sarnia. Though representing Lanark in the House of Assembly from 1836 to 1847, he had moved to Sarnia, where he had subdivided 100 acres for a townsite by 1837. He had taken with him a conspicuous number of half-pay officers and Scottish settlers in a neighbourhood migration.[105]

One of Perth's most famous migrants was John Robson (1824-1892), who went to the Pacific coast in 1859. He founded the first mainland newspaper, the *British Columbian*, at New Westminster in 1861 and served as premier of the province between 1889 and 1892. Movement to the American Midwest and prairies attracted the likes of merchant Alexander McEathron, who left for Chicago in 1849 and eventually settled in South Dakota. W. R. Motherwell, a leader in agricultural education, and born in Perth in 1860, saw the Qu'Appelle Valley for the first time in 1881, and his home, "Lanark Place" is now a national historic site in Saskatchewan. Alexander Morris (1826-1889), a politician and son of merchant William, was lieutenant-governor of Manitoba between 1872 and 1877. The Perth newspapers frequently mentioned departures to the west from the 1880s to the early 1900s. Even cultural heroes from Perth and district, such as writer Charles Mair and artist Edmund Morris made their names in the Canadian West. Rural depopulation from eastern Ontario was even perceived as a social problem at the turn of the century.[106]

A large group from Perth was situated in Winnipeg. In 1881 George Kerr was the health and fire inspector; in 1900 Dr. W.J. Neilson was a member of the legislature from Winnipeg; in 1906 R.L. Richardson was editor of the Winnipeg *Tribune*; and in 1920 P.C. McIntyre was postmaster. In 1906 send-offs from Perth were reported for lawyer J.A. Allen, going to Regina, and Dr. Lafferty, going to Calgary. The Perth *Expositor* commented: "these are only a few of the many who will leave Lanark County for the West this spring." Harvest excursions offered by the CPR encouraged many area farmers or their children to go and see the west for themselves.[107]

Higher education drew Wilmot Burkeman Lane, son of druggist Freeman Lane, to the University of Wisconsin in the 1890s and on to the chair of ethics at Victoria College, University of Toronto, by 1913. Rev. Dr. Robert Campbell (1835-1921) studied in Edinburgh and Glasgow and was a minister in Montreal for more than forty years before becoming moderator of the Presbyterian Church of Canada in 1917. Austin M. Bothwell, son of cooper Thomas Bothwell, became a Rhodes scholar at Oxford in 1906. Perth's excellent public and collegiate educational system propelled many bright students beyond the Tay.[108]

In manufacturing and technology, carriage-maker Matthew Stanley (1845-1922) left behind his considerable factory in 1900 to manage the Birmingham City Tramroad carshops in England. Thomas N. Hicks (1876-1944), son of another carriage-maker, went to McGill in 1902 and pursued an engineering career in New York before returning after retirement. Creighton "Rags" Wilson, engineer son of John Wilson, proprietor of the Hicks House Hotel, became a trapper and fur trader; he lived with his cat on the shore of Great Slave Lake and was buried in a fenced grave overlooking the Mackenzie River in 1929. The drain of its young on many small towns is not a recent phase caused by yellow brick roads to metropolitan centres, but rather part of the transience and mobility of North American life, experienced since the founding of original settlement, which was itself, the result of migration.[109]

Commerce and Industry
There have been several industries and businesses that made major contributions to economic life in Perth and were distinctive in their approach to business during the late nineteenth and early twentieth centuries.

Distilleries[110]
In 1836 Perth had eight taverns, seven stores selling liquor, three distilleries, and a brewery. Its population was only about 1,000, but the local temperance society proclaimed 511 adherents. As well, John A. McLaren declared that "the very acme of heroism with the highlander of Scotland or the well-to-do Irish peasant was the illicit distillation of Mountain Dew for the Scotch or the Potteen for the Irish." Either half the townspeople were heavy drinkers, or the other half were outrageous liars.

Distilling of alcoholic beverages was one of the few local market outlets for farmers' surpluses of grain. While there was local demand for the product, much of it was distilled for export. Among pioneer distillers in Perth were half-pay officers and magistrates Benjamin Deslisle, Henry Graham, Roderick Matheson, and William Morris, whose stills generally handled from 50 to 100 gallons. The government showed little concern for the proliferation of stills or tavern stands, especially since licences for them brought in much-needed tax revenue.

Distilleries were common in pioneer eastern Ontario, but by 1900 only three were still operating, two of them in Perth. Separate companies – Spalding and Stewart Distillery and McLaren's or Perth Distillery – were linked by the Stewart family.

William Locke, from Scotland, operated a brewery and distillery from 1841 on the northwest corner of Gore and Harvey streets by the Gore Street bridge (once known as Locke's bridge). He advertised a 1,400-gallon tub where distiller Peter McEwan, from "the Braes of Breadalbane on the Highlands of Scotland," would mix his "mountain dew." In the 1860s, James Spalding acquired the site; his son

James assumed control in 1872 and formed a partnership in 1879 with Robert Stewart, from Dunkeld, Scotland – Spalding and Stewart. Stewart had been associated with John A. McLaren since 1868. Spalding and Stewart was famous for its brand-name Scotch whiskies "Old Perth" and "Mountain Dew". Stewart remained with the firm until 1910, when he retired at the age of 70. The firm was closed as a result of temperance legislation in 1916. A severe flood on the Tay River weakened a portion of the site in 1926, and two years later, the buildings were torn down.

Robert McLaren was licensed in 1839 with a 40-gallon copper still to produce whiskey. After his death in 1848, the licence went to his wife, Janet, who passed it on to David McLaren by 1852, and he transferred it to Robert Gemmill by 1853. In 1866 John A. McLaren, Robert's son, assumed control. A partnership with Robert Stewart lasting from 1868 to 1879 saw the firm specialize in pure malt whiskey, "the genuine Usquebaugh or small still whiskey so celebrated in Scotland and Ireland." Their brand names were "V.V.O." Canadian Scotch Whiskey and "Old Perth Malt Whiskey." The distillery was on Cockburn Island behind the Town Hall.

The firm employed a complex system of quality manufacturing. Using mostly barley, and distilling only in winter to avoid problems with flies, employees moistened the grain on a very fine mesh above low-pressure steam vents. The process went on day and night, until the sprouted grain was transferred to big tubs, where yeast was added. After fermentation, the mash was put into the still and the condensation rose through coils filtered with hair from the tails of white horses. Workers then transferred the liquid to storage tanks in the bond room. The distillery prided itself on the clarity of water taken from the Tay River, and after the alcohol was extracted from the barley, it fed the remaining mash to the cattle that roamed about Haggart's Island. The distilling process took 30 days, and the use of wood in the malt-making process, rather than peat, as in the old distilleries of Scotland and Ireland, helped create a distinctive flavour.

After John McLaren's death in 1901, the business went to John A. Stewart, son of Robert, who had helped both Spalding and Stewart and the Perth Distillery. The Ontario Temperance Act of 1916 spelled death to the distillery. The site was dismantled in 1918, and the last of its shipment was sent to Quebec and New York in 1919. After the sudden death of John A. Stewart in 1922, his widow gave the land to the town to be used as a park in memory of him. The one industry on which Perth could stake a claim to distinctiveness was closed forever.

Arthur Meighen & Bros.[111]

In 1841, Gordon Meighen of the parish of Boveva, near Londonderry, (Northern) Ireland, emigrated to Perth. Typical of family connection in immigration,

A quiet morning looking south on Foster Street, c. 1900. The general store of Arthur Meighen and Brothers, 1858-1930 is on the right. The awnings along the street create the sense of an arcaded sidewalk. (Courtesy John J. Stewart)

he convinced the widow of his brother Robert to follow with her five sons. Gordon moved farther west; his grandson was Arthur Meighen, prime minister 1920-21 and 1926. But Robert's children stayed in Perth. Eldest son Arthur (1825-1874) opened a general store in 1848, bringing his brothers William (1834-1917) and Robert (1837-1911) into the business in 1867.

In 1867, Arthur Meighen & Bros. moved into "the most substantial cut-stone commercial structure in town," fronting on the northwest corner of Gore and Foster streets. This familiar and surviving structure was once part of a commercial enterprise that spread over an acre of downtown land. The firm handled a significant amount of the region's grain and produce and exported large quantities of local butter and cheese. At the peak of its operation, it had three floors and a basement full of dry goods, millinery, carpets, groceries, and crockery. It was a kind of one-stop shopping based on necessity and convenience. People travelled in from the country to pick up supplies only rarely and needed a considerable array of goods. If Arthur Meighen & Bros. extended credit to customers, they may have had little choice but to buy everything they needed there – and sell everything they produced there as well.

In 1930, after 82 years in business, the firm sold the store. First R. A. Beamish chain store took over the spacious ground floor, and apartments were installed in the floors above. New transportation networks, agricultural markets, and a cash-and-carry system of retail trade had made the small-town general store redundant. An A & P outlet and the Maple Leaf Groceria, Perth's first "self serving" stores, opened on Foster Street in 1930 and 1934, respectively. "Main street" shopping was entering a new era.

John Hart, Bookseller[112]

In 1842, merchant John Hart, Sr., organized a society to bring out settlers to the Perth area from Glasgow. Nine-year-old John Semple Hart (1833-1917), born in Paisley, helped his father set up a store in their new home. Church, education, and books were priorities in the family and in 1850 young John started out on his own as bookseller, on Gore Street, near what is now the Perth Museum.

Hart's was not an ordinary bookstore. It became an intellectual focus for the young community, where people went to read the latest newspapers from London, New York, and Montreal. The store, with counters and shelving of natural wood, was described by the Toronto *Mail* on 14 May 1887 as the dominion's finest bookroom outside Toronto and Montreal. A nephew, W.A. Newman, commented in John Hart's *Diary of a Voyage* (1940): "The store had a great fascination for me and it was a wonderful place for those days, having two front entrances and three plate glass windows with big polished brass hand rails for protection running in front of the windows." John Lovell's *Directory* for several eastern Ontario counties in 1884 called Hart a bookseller and stationer and a "Dealer in English and American Wall Papers, Electro plated Ware, Jewellry, Fancy Goods, Berlin Wools, Musical Instruments & Sheet Music, also Paint, Oils, Glass, Lamp Goods, Garden and Field Seeds."

From the opening of his store in 1850 until about 1914, he published *Hart's Canadian Almanac and Repository of Useful Information and Division Court Directory for the County of Lanark*. This annual publication must have been on every writing desk and store counter in Perth. Hart also introduced the mail flyer in Perth in 1858. *The Gye and Perth Commercial Advertiser*, a free hand-out, included ads and editorials.

After John S. Hart's death in 1917, his son, Will B. Hart, carried on the business until 1928, when the store was sold. The loss of this colourful, eccentric, and vibrant enterprise was a serious blow to Perth's sense of place and stability. The family claimed that the business had become "one of the many victims to the automobile which, to a large degree, has taken the trade of small towns to the big centres."

James Brothers Hardware Store[113]

The James family of Wexford, Ireland, arrived on the Drummond Line, east of Perth, in 1817. By the 1870s, Edward James had moved west into town, where he established a blacksmith shop at North and Drummond streets. His son George S. formed a partnership with Daly Reid in 1892 and opened a hardware store in the old Graham Block (now Royal Bank site) at the corner of Gore and Herriott streets. Lawrence H. James, a brother of George, and a graduate of business college, joined the firm, which had purchased the Robert Lillie foundry in 1899 and operated an iron foundry from the old Stanley carriage-works. The firm further diversified into manufacturing by adding a machine shop and repair facility. Not only did James & Reid make and sell many of their own goods, they were aggressive in providing their own delivery wagons to service outlying districts.

In 1910, the company purchased its main competitor, Warren & McCarthy, and took over its location, which had been at the corner of Gore and Foster streets since 1880. At a machine shop next to the store, and at its foundry, it manufactured "New Century plows," sleighs, door springs, roof ladders, rink scrapers, fire escapes, sewer castings, shovels, fireplace baskets, pig rings (more than 500,000 in 1895), water tanks, and clothes hangers. Many of its inventions and gadgets were created by a gifted mechanic, Tommy Thompson. After D. W. Reid's retirement in 1921, the firm was called James Brothers.

In addition to the hardware store, foundry, and machine shop, James Brothers started a sports department (before the turn of the century selling 100 bicycles in a year, many of their own design and manufacture), car dealership, coal and wood yard, and poster advertising business, and it ran two service stations and garages. On their own, the James family operated the old hockey rink and, at the end of the Second World War, started Jamesville, a subdivision (Perth's first suburb) between the town and Highway 7. By the 1950s, the firm had 50 people on the payroll and considered its market to be within a 30 mile radius of Perth.

The James & Reid operation established an important local link between manufacturing and retail sales. It made a lot of what it sold, its name was on its product, it delivered to people's doors, and it repaired its goods on site. James Brothers effectively bridged the gap between an economy based on the horse and carriage and one based on the automobile. It grasped the critical importance of servicing the growing recreational and tourist community on the Rideau Lakes; it was building and selling motorboats soon after 1900 and was promoting "50 lakes within 50 miles" as an incentive to tourists. Besides having a well-equipped fishing section in its store, it sponsored for many years a big-fish contest that sustained widespread interest. In 1952, under the direction of new partner and

Victoria Hall, or the Malloch House, now the Great War Memorial Hospital, c. 1920s. The residence of John Glass Malloch (1806-1873) was erected in 1858. Judge Malloch came to Perth in 1834 to practise law and was appointed Judge of the District Court of Bathurst in 1842, later the County Court of Lanark. He had purchased the park lot of his father-in-law, the Rev. William Bell, and the site was developed as a hospital from 1922. (Postcard, collection of author)

George's son Alan E. James, the company sent 3,000 fishing calendars to customers in the United States. A lot of the original character of the James Brothers store was lost in modernization and after Alan sold the store to David Weir in 1974. The name, however, is still a familiar landmark on Perth's famous corner, where each building still serves the purpose for which it was built in the nineteenth century.

Late Victorian Splendour

Some of the town's most striking buildings above North Street were erected in the late Victorian era. The 25-acre park lots were useful for descendants of the original owners or speculators who had bought them. The early scheme of grants did little to facilitate growth. Half-pay officers Col. Josiah Taylor, James Adamson, and William Hunter had subdivided portions of their lands just beyond North Street; much later the lots provided space on which wealthier inhabitants could erect new homes and spread their lawns and gardens. Except on Taylor's park lot 8 south of Wilson Street, expansion was reserved largely for the middle and upper classes.[114]

Vestiges of these park lots are still visible, especially where Isabella Street

Restricted to the north and south by wetlands, Perth in 1874 clusters around the east-west corridors of Gore, Drummond and Beckwith streets. Note artisans' shops, hotels, and merchant houses and industrial activity at mills on Haggart Island, distilleries on or near Cockburn Island, tanneries at the Tay Basin, and William Pink's furniture factory belching smoke. Sawn lumber is ready for shipment on the Perth branch of the Brockville and Ottawa Railway. (Detail from Bird's Eye View of Perth, 1874, NA, NMC 4304)

forms a boundary between the first and second tiers. The park lot granted to Rev. William Bell and acquired by his son-in-law, John Glass Malloch, is the site of Victoria Hall, built in 1858, now anchoring the Great War Memorial Hospital. The wonderful grounds at Nevis Cottage, the next park lot west of the hospital, was originally granted to John A. Murdoch, an assistant to the Lanark settlement superintendent. The Links O' Tay golf course is spread over the old Matheson farm, part of park lot 6.

The town plan ensured compact and orderly groupings or precincts of housing stock. The boom of 1880, which saw many of the Victorian structures erected on Drummond Street, also brought about a wide range of residential accommodation built in the lee of new industry and railway development followed by another building boom around 1902 to 1905 and 1911. Other contributing factors included relatively accessible forests for building materials, local clay, an early brick-making establishment, and, most important, a series of very successful limestone and sandstone quarries near town. The Hughes Quarry, operating at the turn of the century, provided material for new buildings and introduced a new lexicon of building material into the town's stone landscape. The dressed stone, with darker quoins and banding, and the distinctive purple veins running through the bedding planes attest to the mason's skills and Edwardian tastes for overstatement. George Thomas Martin, a Smiths Falls architect, seems to have favoured this stone; his stylish Romanesque treatment for the House of Industry, St. John's Convent, and the Code complex enriched the town.

The early 1880s and turn of the century were economic boom times. A noted expression of this affluence is the complex of buildings developed by Thomas Alfred Code, which dominates almost an entire block of Perth's downtown core, from the corner of Gore Street along Herriott Street and up Wilson Street. Un-like Matheson's tight, fortress-like development at Gore and Foster, built adja-cent to the street with walled internal courtyards, the Code complex dramati-cally reflects the "City Beautiful" movement, with buildings set out almost as if on public display. It includes his grand Edwardian residence Kininvie, a stone boomtown-fronted duplex, the imposing three-storey Royal Bank Building, and his Mill. The Mill itself is actually a collage of five different buildings dating from

House of Industry, c. 1910. George Martin of Smiths Falls designed this fine Romanesque structure in 1903 with stone quarried in Elmsley and Bathurst townships. In the first dec-ade of the 20th century counties were encouraged to build Houses of Refuge or Industry to provide the poor, destitute and elderly with shelter and care. (Postcard, collection of author)

1842. Known as The Code Custom Wool Mills, the 1902 wing presented a striking public facade and offices. The use of distinctive Hughes stone unifies this composition of buildings and landscapes, overlooking the Tay River.

Thomas Allan Code, who started his woollen mill in Innisville, was one of several entrepreneurs active in eastern Ontario's woollen industry. He moved to Perth in 1876, and by 1883 he had acquired the old Kilpatrick tannery at Herriott and Wilson. The continuing production at Code Felt Ltd is a legacy to the founder, who spent 60 years in business in Perth. In the 1890s, Lawrence Gemmill moved his woollen mills from Port Elmsley to the corner of Rogers Road and Harvey Street on account of a town bonus and a better supply of water. The Codes eventually absorbed his operation.

Kininvie built in 1906 for textile manufacturer Thomas A. Code (1854-1937). His handsome mill structures, house, and the Code block at Gore Street transformed Herriott Street. (Postcard, c. 1910, collection of author)

CHAPTER SIX

Victorian Life in Perth

The half-pay officers and administrators who founded Perth may have imitated the social models of a civil and landed gentry, but they were also touched by the realities of their time and place. Logging bees, spring drives, quilting sessions, barn raisings, dances, and sugaring off helped form folk life as effectively as traditions from the homeland, based on harvest festivals, patriotic celebrations, and ethnic and religious ceremonies. Scottish, Irish, and English traditions helped shape Perth's cultural atmosphere, but Canadian influences moulded the identity of organizations and the pursuit of social interaction, culture, pleasure, and recreation.

Culture

Perth was well served by early newspapers, including the *Bathurst* (later Perth) *Courier*, begun by Malcolm Cameron in 1834, which survives today, as well as the Perth *Expositor*, which published from 1860 to 1936 before being absorbed by the *Courier*. The early papers tended at first to derive their stories from larger . dailies and gave limited space to local non-political events, but with the increasing availability of other newspapers handling world and national events, eventually they began to look closer to home. In 1847, the Perth *Courier* commented on the "thirst for knowledge" generated when the Perth Debating Society met at a tea party at Mr. Quail's Temperance House, where members were entertained with vocal and instrumental music and recitations. The local papers began to run social columns that described parties, teas, meetings, weddings, funerals, visitors, picnics, sports, dances, rumours, and notable disasters. These often-snobbish en-

Perth Library, c. 1914. A distinctive feature in small towns throughout North America is the local library, erected with the support of the Carnegie Foundation. The Perth Scientific and Literary Society, formed in 1906 to obtain a Carnegie grant, erected this Beaux Arts building on Gore Street in 1907. A fire in 1980 destroyed the collection, but not the structure. The library now has new quarters on Herriott Street. (Postcard, collection of author)

tries made for great reading, especially from the 1870s to the 1920s.[115]

The early ministers of religion encouraged literacy and libraries to raise moral and intellectual standards. A meeting held in 1832 to raise subscriptions for a library met with little success. A Mechanics Institute begun in 1844 subscribed to the most influential dailies, journals, and magazines, and it joined with the Public Library, started by Rev. William Bell in 1847, to create a public reading room. Both institutions later flagged, until the Mechanics Institute was reorganized in 1881, again with responsibility for the library. About 1900, J. K. Robertson remembered the Mechanics Hall as the town's main recreational building, where checkers was the popular game.[116]

John Hart's bookstore, begun in 1850, provided the community with an excellent source of books and reading materials for over seventy-five years. Charles Mair, born in Lanark and son of a Perth merchant family, provided a literary hero to the community as a poet and a founder of the Canada First Movement, in the same way that Edmund Morris did so for artist's circles. Both became famous for their depiction of frontier western life in Canada. The Perth Scientific and Literary Society was formed in 1906 to lobby the Carnegie Foundation for a public library, which was erected in Beaux Arts style on Gore Street in 1907. This library was destroyed by fire in 1980, but a new library was erected soon afterward on Herriott Street.[117]

In the 1820s, John W. Adams, precentor in Rev. Bell's church, led the singing of hymns on Sunday. He launched a "school for instruction in the elements and practice of local music" and spent over sixty years teaching music in Perth. In 1849, for six shillings, eight pence (exclusive of candles and fuel), Adams would teach two nights a week for four months. The community was rewarded with a concert of sacred music by approximately eighty singers at the Free Church early in April 1850. By 1851, Perth had its own music hall, on the second floor of 53 D'Arcy Street. A ballroom was located on the second floor of the Town Hall, erected in 1863; the professional singer Madame Anna Bishop opened the build-ing officially in September 1864. One would have imagined a different crowd at the London Comedy and Burlesque Company's productions of 'Faint Heart', 'Loan of a Lover' and 'Rough Diamond' in 1869, but it was sponsored by the Good Templars of Perth.[118]

Anna M. Allan remembered Perth as having a rich singing tradition, encour-aged by the churches and the availability of the music hall. 'Penny Readings' were a popular form of entertainment. In the winter of 1870, they were held fort-nightly to raise money for a piano. On Friday evening, 4 March 1870, H. D. Shaw chaired a Penny Reading (it actually cost 5 cents) that included instru-mental music by the 'String Band', choral music by Dr. Nichol and chorus, and readings by Rev. Stephenson, John Haggart, J. W. Douglas, Malcolm Cameron, W. J. Pink and S. R. Hart. Highlights included "Maggie's Secret" sung by Mrs. P. Ryan, "Bonnie New Moon" by Miss Buell, other songs by Mrs. Seeley and Miss McDonnell, and duets by Mrs. Ryan, and E. O'Brien, Miss Mowat, and Miss Hicks. These amateur productions reduced the need for paid singers. Olivia Campbell, daughter of a fiddler who "made the blood tingle," went on to a sing-ing career in New York City.[119]

Sports and Leisure

The arduous tasks and long hours of work left pioneer settlers little time or en-ergy for leisure pursuits, and the central role of clergy also discouraged pleasures not deemed to improve character or morality, especially on the Sabbath, the only day of rest from work.

Sporting activities surfaced, however, at militia musters and on fair days. Horse racing was a favourite. In 1829, Rev. William Bell commented: "The Bench of Magistrates at the recommendation of the Grand Jury made an order against horse racing in the streets, which had become quite common, endanger-ing lives. But on the first day of the Fair there was racing as usual, with 8 Magis-trates present and betting on the horses."[120]

Early fire companies in Perth set a competitive tone. The East Ward's Fountain company, wearing blue jackets and white trousers, and the West Ward's Union company, sporting red shirts and black trousers, competed in the proficiency of their fire-fighting. In the 1850s, the two groups, containing as many as 50 to 60 members, even set fire to abandoned buildings to test their abilities. This recreational arson came to a halt after George Miller, an esteemed citizen and fire-fighter, was accidentally burned when the companies torched the old abandoned Catholic church to see who would be better at putting out the fire.[121]

Cricket was perhaps the first organized sport in Perth, with games being played against Almonte, Merrickville, and Smiths Falls in the early 1860s. At Confederation, lacrosse and baseball were being played. When a sport was received, refined, or invented, Canadians created some semblance of order and then competed with neighbouring communities or localities. By waterway, rail, or road, Perth teams visited and hosted other Lanark County and eastern Ontario teams. Socials were held to raise money for teams, and community pride was at stake in a host of tournaments. Team sports in Perth were played at the

Perth junior baseball club, 1916. From the 1860s with cricket and lacrosse, and later baseball and hockey, local sports teams flourished in club, community and inter-county competition. (Courtesy Rusty White)

South Lanark Exhibition Grounds, Perth, Ont.

The South Lanark exhibition grounds were located at Fairholm Park off Wilson Street when this photo was taken before 1912. The fairgrounds reminded citizens of the symbiotic relationship between the town and rural community. Fairs in Perth date back to at least 1824 and the annual fair is held on the first weekend in September. (Postcard, courtesy Rusty White collection)

athletic grounds at the site of the present Perth Fair, established in 1885 to accommodate track and field sports.

As Canada's official national sport, lacrosse had its origins in a native game introduced by the Iroquois. The formation of the National Lacrosse Association in Kingston in 1867 led to a proliferation of clubs in small towns. The Perth Chokecherries were formed in 1890, reorganized as the Perth Crescents Lacrosse Club in 1893. They played in eastern Ontario and northern New York, winning the Ottawa Valley championship four times between 1900 and 1910.[122]

In the 1870s, informal and organized baseball swept Ontario. The first game in Perth may have been played with six-man teams at the Victoria Day invitational firemen's celebration in 1860. It became a standard summer pastime with competition in several rural and regional leagues. A semi-professional team played in the early 1930s in the St. Lawrence League, and Rusty White played on the Perth Royals, which survived a few years before 1940 in the Canadian-American Class "C" League. In the 1920s, women's softball became a competitive sport, and Perth teams competed throughout eastern Ontario.[123]

Ice hockey was a natural sport for eastern Ontario. Aside from ice on the Tay

River, Perth had a covered skating rink as early as 1863, and the old military drill hall also had a rink. The arena at Herriott and Beckwith streets (built 1899, now demolished) had an ice surface 70 ft. wide and 170 ft. long and was considered the finest in the region. The Perth team, the Crescents, won the Group Two title of the Ontario Hockey Association in 1904 and qualified to play in the Stanley Cup playoffs. The Crescents were defeated by the Toronto Marlboros, and the cup went to the legendary Ottawa Silver Seven. Frank McLaren, a superb athlete in both lacrosse and hockey, played for teams in Toronto; he and his six brothers in Perth could take on any team.

Religion and Churches

The large, highly rural parishes and circuits of early Perth, discussed in chapter 4, gave way in Victorian times to urban charges with more stability and a desire to create finer and larger houses of worship. By the 1880s, all the major denominations in Perth boasted buildings of worship with medieval motifs, largely in Gothic form – a style that dominated Ontario's Victorian churches. Religion was at the core of social organization, influencing education, charity, social clubs, and, in many cases, business dealings. In the dawning era of the social gospel, community salvation and the search for heaven on earth became part of a moral crusade. Perth contributed missionaries to far reaches of the British Empire to extoll the virtues of Christianity. However, in a traditional society, groups such as the Orange Lodge, which sustained ancient religious-political passions into the new era, continued their potential for discord in the community (L.O.L. 115 is still located on Gore Street).

In the census of 1881, Perth, with a population of 2,467, reported 725 adherents to one form or another of Presbyterianism; 671 Anglicans; 520 Roman Catholics; 343 Methodists; 133 Baptists; 20 Brethren; 12 Disciples; and 5 others.

Presbyterian

William Bell's First Presbyterian Church, built in 1819, used to stand at the northeast corner of Drummond and Halton streets. Rev. Bell established the traditional kirk session which policed and disciplined the congregation. Church elders would sit in judgment on fornication, alcoholism, and Sabbath desecration, as well as irregular marriage and elopement, drunkenness and fighting, slander and quarrelling, absenteeism, fraud, and business-related misdemeanours.

Rev. Bell led a Secession congregation, one of the many divisions that characterized Presbyterianism. In 1899, Rev. Dr. Robert Campbell remembered Bell as being slow and deliberate, clear-cut, and easily understood, and "his prayers were simple and beautiful." While his preaching lacked emotion and enthusiasm, "he stood head and shoulders above his contemporaries in the preaching field, in broad culture and intellectual attainments."[124] Seceders tended to be democratic in temper, often radical in politics, and strong in personal piety. Some members of Bell's congregation would delete democratic and add autocratic for him, as an anonymous letter claimed in the 1820s: "are you not aware that a very large portion of the Presbyterians ... in consequence of your unpleasant temper and tyrannical conduct, are dissatisfied with your ministrations."[125] Owing in part to Bell's eccentricities there emerged ample support from the likes of such luminaries as William Morris and Roderick Matheson for a minister from the established Church of Scotland by the 1820s.

The Church of Scotland was under a strong Calvinist influence, where raising the standards of literature and learning was sacrosanct. The Rev. Thomas C. Wilson arrived in 1830 and built St. Andrews Church at the corner of Drummond and Craig streets, east of the Court House, in 1832. By 1835, Bell had returned to the Church of Scotland, and the Presbyterians were assembled into Bell's "First Presbyterian Congregation" and Wilson's "the Congregation of St. Andrew." In 1841, Bell's church had 200 adherents to Wilson's 400. Shortly before Bell's death in 1857, the congregations united. After St. Andrews was destroyed by fire in 1923, the new church was built by 1928 at the corner of North and Drummond streets.

The "Disruption of 1843" saw a split from the Church of Scotland Synod and creation of the Canadian Free Church, based on a transatlantic movement for the defence of evangelical theology, congregational rights, and the Headship of Christ over His church. Quite a few Presbyterians withdrew from Bell's church and St. Andrews to create Knox Presbyterian in 1844. In less than 20 years, the Free Kirk became the fourth-largest denomination in Canada.[126]

In Neil Robertson's "Early Days of Perth," the author described one family that had seceded; its dog had always gone to church with the family and had his sleeping place under one of the pews. He refused to secede. He followed the family rig as before into town, but as it repaired to Knox Church, he wended his way to his old seat in the old church.[127] A frame building erected in 1845 at the corner of Gore and D'Arcy streets was replaced in 1854 by the present freestone church which underwent modifications in 1899 and 1964. After the Methodist congregation joined that of Knox Presbyterian at the time of Union in 1925, Knox was renamed St. Paul's United Church in 1926.

Church of England

A loyal and ordered population was the basis of a Christian society, according to Anglicans. The established Church of England eventually found itself disestablished in the cultural plurality of the province. When Rev. Michael Harris

St. James Anglican Church, c. 1905. The present structure of this Royal Charter Church was opened in 1861 and designed in part by Fuller and Jones, who were architects of Canada's original centre-block Parliament building. The tower and spire were added in 1888. (Postcard, collection of author)

arrived in Perth in 1819, the notion of Upper Canada becoming a utopian bastion of Anglicanism was still very real, but declining. In spite of the best efforts of Bishop John Strachan and colonial authorities in York (Toronto), Anglicanism could not sustain the established status that it enjoyed in England and Ireland. Indeed, the church in Ontario moved closer to Presbyterianism and Methodism, emphasizing Protestant culture. By the 1850s, the Church of England was evolving into a self-governing, self-supporting institution.[128]

The first St. James Anglican Church was erected in 1822 as a frame building, 50 by 40 feet, at its present site at Drummond and Harvey streets. St. James is one of the few Royal Chapter Churches in Canada, a status granted in the 1830s by William IV and allowing servers and the choir to wear scarlet cassocks. Rev. A. Pyne, who served between 1853 and 1857, arranged for plans by a Toronto firm for a new church. Messrs. Thomas Fuller and Chilion Jones, who built Parliament's original centre block, altered these plans. The Gothic-style church opened in 1861; a spire and tower were added in 1888 as a gift from Senator Peter McLaren. King Arnoldi, another architect from Ottawa, designed the rectory, built in 1875.

Roman Catholic

The first Roman Catholic church in Perth, built on the west side of Harvey between Beckwith and Drummond in 1820, burned in 1853, but not before the rise of the magisterial St. John's at the end of Brock Street. Constructed probably by Irish stonemasons and influenced by Rt. Rev. Patrick Phalen, co-adjutor of the diocese of Kingston from 1843 to 1857, St. John's was central to a large Scots and Irish Catholic community. The graceful St. John's Convent, which housed the Sisters of Providence of St. Vincent de Paul, was built in 1905 by George Martin of Smiths Falls.[129]

The Catholic church faced an uphill battle for recognition and respect in an area so dominated by Protestant settlers. Divisions within the Scots, Irish, and French congregation paled beside the determined opposition that Catholics faced among Irish Protestant's nervous about the liberty that the church enjoyed compared to the familiar penal codes of Ireland. Especially during the famine emigration years in the 1840s, when arriving Irish Catholics were distinctly more poorer, the church and its people suffered some discrimination. Fallout from strained relations between the English-speaking Protestant majority in Upper Canada/Ontario and the French speaking Catholic majority in Lower Canada/Quebec contributed to misunderstanding in communities such as Perth, with a large Orange population. In elections to the present day, Perth's East Ward is largely Catholic and Liberal, and the West Ward is Protestant and Conservative.

St. John's Church, described as "one of the noblest remaining from the mid-

St. John's Convent, c. 1910. The Sisters of Providence of St. Vincent de Paul arrived in
Perth in 1892 and they erected St. John's Convent in 1905. Designed by George Martin of
Smiths Falls and built from local sandstone, it served as a high school from 1985 until 1992
when the new school was completed. (Postcard, collection of author)

century" anchored a Catholic community that began to dominate the East Ward
of Perth. Catholics doubled in number between 1881 and 1901, from 520 to
1,006, and between 1900 and 1920, St. John's was the largest congregation in
Perth. It has stabilized at around 20 percent of the population who declare religious denomination. Farrell Hall, owned and operated by the Knights of
Columbus since 1964, remains one of the busiest community centres in Perth
and serves a wide spectrum of its citizens.

Methodist

Old-style Methodism defined the sacred as an immediate and omnipresent real-
ity that intervened in the affairs of the world. Following the preachings of John
Wesley, Methodism was an offshoot from the Church of England. The presence
of the hand of God in human affairs lent passion to a church where religious experience could be intense and dramatic. Revivalism and evangelism were important ingredients in the development of Methodism. However, as the church grew
more established, it moderated its approach to religious experience.[130]

A Methodist log chapel was erected in 1820; it was replaced on the west side
of Gore Street in 1835 and enlarged in 1856. Perth's Methodists were apparently
of the British Wesleyan tradition, which saw itself originally as a movement and
only later as a church. In spite of attempts at union, the British-inspired

Wesleyans and the American-influenced Episcopals found little in common, especially in a town with such strong British origins. The stone building for Asbury Methodist Church was erected in the Gothic style in time for the Methodist union of 1884. Following the union of the Asbury and Knox churches in 1925 as part of the new United Church, the building was sold in 1928 to the dominion government, which lopped off the two steeples in 1935. After its duty as an armoury, the Free Methodists rescued the building in 1965 for the purpose for which it was built.[131]

Baptist

The Baptists of Perth owe their origins to the settlement of Scottish Baptists in eastern Upper Canada. Although the church was late getting under way in Perth, it became a stable fifth denomination in the community. Baptists insisted on restricting communion to immersed believers, and they believed strongly in local autonomy and independence from central control.

The First Baptist Meeting House was built on D'Arcy Street in 1842, followed by the present brick building of 1888 designed by Langley and Burke of Toronto. During construction of the church, services were held in the "music hall" on the second floor of the stone block next door. The Baptist Church was originally organized in 1842 by Rev. Robert Alexander Fyfe (1816-1878), who spent two terms in Perth and is considered one of the spiritual founders of McMaster University, through his establishment of the Canadian Literary Institute at Woodstock in 1860. Another former pastor, Rev. Thomas Henderson, convinced Alexander Melville Bell to emigrate from Scotland; Bell brought his son, Alexander Graham, to Canada, where he developed the telephone. The latter Bell placed one of his earliest phones in 1876 in the D'Arcy building next to the church, where Rev. Henderson's son-in-law, Dr. J. F. Kennedy, could be connected with his dentist's office on Foster Street.[132]

Others Denominations and Faiths

The Perth Corps of the Salvation Army is more than a century old and operates its chapel on Gore Street and a store for clothing on Foster Street. The Glad Tidings Pentacostal Church opened in Perth in 1935, under Rev. Burgess, who led the congregation until 1952, taking time out during the war to work as a military chaplain. The Pentacostal church is rooted in evangelical tradition, and the community in Perth is part of the Pentacostal Assemblies of Canada. The Brethren have deep roots in Perth for over a century and used to hold services in the McMartin House, which also served as St. John's Memorial Hall for the Catholic community. The New Testament Church currently holds services at the McMartin House.

On 14 June 1925, a joint communion service of Asbury and Knox congregations, numbering 475, took place. The basis of Union was read to both congregations early in 1926, and a decision was made to establish services at the old Knox Church, which became St. Paul's United. While many Presbyterians would oppose union, by 1931 the United Church was a few shy of the largest congregation in Perth, with 1,125 adherents, and it has been the dominant church since.[133]

After the Second World War, for about 20 years, a synagogue served about a dozen local Jewish families in the stone building, formerly the Patterson Hotel, at Drummond and Harvey streets.

Public Education

As we saw in chapter 4, passing of the School Act of 1841 began a transformation of public education in the province. In 1851, the Perth Common School and the Perth Grammar School amalgamated and erected the Perth Public School, an elegant stone building opened on the south side of Foster Street in 1852. John Kerr remembered the austere discipline of the school in the 1850s and 1860s: "At an early age I was taken to the Perth Public School and handed over to the tender mercies – and the 'tawse' – of the principal thereof, a bully and a tyrant, if ever there was one. During my sojurn at the public and grammar schools, I passed through the hands (and when I mean 'hands', I mean *hands*, not only in a literary, but in a literal sense) of some dozen teachers. Heavy hands they were, most of them!"[134]

The old stone school survived for a century, with several additions. In 1949, the Queen Elizabeth School was built in the East Ward; in 1951, Stewart School was completed in the West Ward. The old school became redundant and was razed in 1952; the hockey rink now stands in its place.

In 1875, Perth High School emerged from the old grammar school division of the public school. A handsome Second Empire building designed by King Arnoldi of Ottawa opened a year later. In 1880, the school became the third collegiate institute in eastern Ontario. Later expansion reflected its growing role as a district institution. Eventually the original building disappeared in the path of "progress" in 1972.[135]

John Alexander Murdoch, an assistant to the superintendent of the Lanark settlement, was the earliest Catholic teacher in Perth. A Roman Catholic separate school was founded in 1856 near the church. The two-room school was replaced in 1890 with a four-room edifice. The existing three-storey structure was opened in 1927. In 1892, the Sisters of Providence of St. Vincent de Paul took over direction of the school. At the conclusion of their teaching duties in 1985, the Sisters turned over the convent to the secondary school, which had started

The Perth High School was created in 1875 to replace the outmoded district grammar school. In 1876, a proud new school designed by Ottawa architect King Arnoldi in the Second Empire style, graced Victoria Street. An increasing school population encouraged several additions until 1972, when the old structure became sadly redundant and was demolished. (Archives of Ontario, S17921 Acc.6923)

grade 9 classes in 1950. In 1985 the Lanark, Leeds and Grenville Separate School Board assumed control and developed a full high school program. A new St. John's High School opened in 1992.[136]

Post-secondary education settled in Perth only in the late twentieth century. Algonquin College was an important addition to the Perth community, when a campus opened in 1968, with classes originally being held in Perth and District Collegiate Institute. The present Lanark Campus on highway 43 at the edge of town, opened in December 1970.

Rebellions and Wars

Since the founding of the Perth military settlement, its residents have taken part in fighting domestic rebellions and foreign wars. Sir Henry George Elliot, born in Perth in 1826, was a second lieutenant in the Royal Navy Light Infantry at the sieges of Sebastopol and Balaclava during the Crimean War and later became a colonial officer in South Africa. Herbert Taylor Reade (1828-1897), son of half-pay officer and surgeon George Hume Reade, won the Victoria Cross at the siege of Delhi during the Indian Mutiny of 1857. Reade, an assistant surgeon in the 61st Regiment of the British Army, was the first Canadian-born recipient of the British Empire's highest military award. He went on to serve in Africa and the West Indies and was appointed surgeon-general of the British Army in 1886.

He and his brother, John By Cole Reade, who had been a surgeon in the Crimean War, the Afghan War, and the Indian Mutiny, were appointed in 1895 honorary surgeons in the Royal Household.[137]

Patrick Spence, a Perth livery stable operator and stage-coach driver, supplied horses to the Union Army during the US Civil War. D. George McMartin served as an officer in the Union Army. In 1866 the 3rd Company of Perth Rifles in the 42nd Brockville Battalion was stationed at Fort Wellington in Prescott during the Fenian scare.

In 1870, John A. Kerr (1851-1940), later town clerk, was in No. 7 Company, 1st Ontario Rifles, which marched west with Colonel Wolseley's Red River expedition against Louis Riel. Kerr was part of a group of regimental choristers asked to serenade Manitoba's newly appointed lieutenant-governor, Adams George Archibald, in Fort Frances during the trek west. He also joined the Manitoba constabulary and was one of three officers who in 1873 arrested Riel's former adjutant-general, Ambroise Lepine, who was later convicted for executing Thomas Scott. Kerr's son, George T., served in the US Navy, Strathcona's Horse in the Boer War, and as sergeant-major of the Lanark and Renfrew Scottish Regiment.[138]

There was no regimental chorus singing in Perth after the second Riel rebellion. Perth's first martyr was Lieut. Alexander W. Kippen, DLS, killed in the battle of Batoche on 12 May 1885. Kippen was a surveyor with the Hudson's Bay Co. and volunteered to join the Dominion Surveyors' Intelligence Corps as a scout under Capt. J.S. Dennis. He died in his first engagement, shortly after reaching the camp of Gen. Frederick Middleton. Perth sentiment was aroused at his death and after a remarkable ceremony and burial, a large monument was erected in Elmwood cemetery.[139]

J. Moran wrote a poem on the funeral of Lieut. Kippen, on 13 June 1885; it included the following stanza:

And your town who claims him proudly,
Fair and hopeful town of Perth,
Who to-day bewails him loudly,
You were proud to give him birth,
But be prouder of his ashes;
Make his monument to shine
In a brilliancy of flashes
E're the morning guilds the pine...[140]

J.K. Robertson's *Tayville* gives a thrilling account of the impact of the Boer War on turn-of-the-century Perth. He describes the local response to the relief of Ladysmith: on 1 March 1900 the town celebrated the rescue of the British garrison there with a spontaneous parade starting at the high school and winding its way through town amid a snow storm.

> In the evening, at a mass meeting held in the Town Hall, standing room was at a premium, and enthusiasm continued unabated. The Regimental band played popular and patriotic airs; Mr. Henry Morgan [Taylor], the local magistrate with the pleasing baritone voice once again sang "The Soldiers of the Queen," the whole audience joining in the chorus; "Rule Britannia" was sung by the male quartette with such a spirit that for full five minutes the applause and cheering continued. Speeches were made by the Mayor and all the town councillors, and, by a standing vote, it was unaminously and enthusiastically decided to cable Her Majesty the Queen the following message: "Tayville [Perth] extends congratulations and rejoices in the brilliant success of British soldiers. God save the Queen."[141]

Enthusiasm for the British Empire, and Canada's role within it, was central to Perth's world-view. Robertson wrote about the town's peculiar military flavour and how this could be expressed in something as simple as a drill-shed. The shed sat in a stategic position near the railway station, designed to impress strangers as they arrived: "it was possible to miss the old cannon of 1812 which stood in front of the Court House, and, as vistors were not always taken to the cemetery, the magnificent monument, surmounted by a life-size figure of one [Alexander Kippen] who had fallen in the North-West Rebellion of 1885, was frequently overlooked – but, walking or riding, the drill-shed could not be avoided."[142]

Orange Day parade on Gore Street, c. 1900. Orange Day and St. Patrick's Day had their traditional parades, but there were other excuses for having parades that brought out banners, flags, special carriages, politicians, the militia, and the Citizens Band, including the celebration of Imperial victories, civic holidays, and the circus coming to town. (Courtesy John J. Stewart)

CHAPTER SEVEN

Twentieth-Century Growth

An Expanding Economy

Despite general prosperity before the First World War, Perth's population remained stable between 1901 and 1911, when it stood at 3,588. Rural depopulation and urban centralization were having their effects. In 1904, the CPR car works burned on Sherbrooke Street; production was moved to Montreal by 1905, with the loss of from 200 to 400 jobs. Observing the trend of modern business toward centralization, Rev. Ross commented in 1905: "it is a matter of deep regret to all its old citizens that the town's somewhat belated and spasmodic efforts to recover the lost ground have not met with the success they deserved."[143]

John A. Stewart (1867-1922) led an aggressive campaign to attract industry in Perth. John was born in Renfrew in 1867 and taken to Perth as an infant. He was apprenticed as a mercantile clerk at the age of 12 and returned to school at 22 to take up law. After setting up a practice with associates in a law firm (Rogers and Stewart, now O'Donnell Dulmage Bond March & Anderson on Market Street), he entered business by attracting to Perth, and later serving as president of two American firms, the Henry K. Walmpole Co. (1905) and the Andrew Jergens Company (1917), both still in operation with greatly expanded facilities. He acquired and became president of the Perth Shoe Co. in 1912 (formerly Winn Co. and still operating as a branch of Brown Shoes) and successfully operated the famous McLaren Distillery from 1901 until termination by the Ontario Temperance Act in 1916. He also became owner of the local Conservative newspaper, the Perth

Expositor. At one time the shoe, cosmetic, and pharmaceutical factories formed an industrial block by the old CPR works on Sherbrooke Street on the northeast side of town, near the railway station, where Jergens is still maintained.[144]

Encouraged by Stewart, the town council offered bonuses of $25,000 to entice carpet, shoe and pharmaceutical industries from Guelph, Milton, and Toronto between 1905 and 1911. The provincial legislature blocked the Winn Shoe Co. from moving to Perth in 1905 but later relented and 11 freight cars and 60 employees arrived from Milton in 1911. Soon after the entire Toronto plant of Walmpole was shifted from Toronto to Perth in 1905, John Stewart and W. E. Danner bought out the original American owners, in 1907. In 1912, the Andrew Jergens Co. of Cincinnati, which had been working in conjunction with H. K. Walmpole in the United States, transferred its Canadian business to Walmpole at Perth. In 1917, Jergens began developing its Sherbrooke Street property with Walmpole, but now separately recognized as the Andrew Jergens Co. Stewart was secretary treasurer of the new enterprise.[145] Council also helped escort the Guelph Carpet Works to Perth in 1911 with a town loan guarantee. Failure of the Guelph plant coincided with a fire at Boyd Caldwell & Co. in Lanark to encourage Thomas Boyd Caldwell to build the Taybank woollen mills on the site in 1917. They became Tayside Textiles in 1925 and employed up to 100 people before closing in 1966, and after attempts by Brewster Fabrics and Collies to reopen the plant, it was demolished in 1986.[146] By providing capital, manipulating town bonus and loan schemes, and utilizing the properties of the old CPR works, Stewart delivered a new era of industrial plants to Perth.

Stewart was active in several local clubs and offices, including mayor, served in Arthur Meighen's cabinet in 1920-21, was the high chief ranger of the Canadian Order of Foresters 1903-17, and was the founder of the Perth Improvement Co. His sudden death at age 55 in 1922 robbed the community of its most energetic and successful business leader. A public school and the town's island park

John Alexander Stewart (1867-1922), son of Perth's famous distiller, Robert, of Dunkfeld, Scotland, was a lawyer, politician and industrialist. He served 2 terms as mayor of Perth, owned McLaren's distilley, and attracted Henry K. Walmpole Co. to Perth in 1905, followed by Jergens. He aquired the Perth Shoe Co. (now Brown Shoe) and became a Director of Frost and Woods in Smiths Falls. He was the Minister of Railways and Canals in Arthur Meighen's cabinet of 1920-21. His wife, Jessie Mabel Henderson (1869-1956), became National President of the IODE and gave Stewart park to the town. (Courtesy, Perth Museum)

Perth Shoe Co. factory, c. 1920s. After the loss of the CPR car-works in 1904, Perth of-
fered industrial bonuses or loans to factories to locate by the railway yards on Sherbrooke
Street. Winn Shoes, later Perth Shoe Co., and presently Brown Shoes, was attracted to
Perth in 1911. The area was home base for four factories before 1920 including Walmpole,
Jergens, Guelph Carpets and the shoe company. (Postcard, collection of author)

commemorates his legacy. The park was donated by his widow, Jessie Mabel
(Henderson), a former president of the Imperial Order of the Daughters of the
Empire in Canada. The Stewarts had lived in the old Henderson residence,
Thuresson Place, on Drummond Street, now Perth Manor.[147]

Perth offered a safe, stable environment for expansion of these American interests in Canada, a precursor to the branch plant influx after 1945. Wages were
lower than in other parts of the province, and unions had little strength – indeed,
were actively discouraged. Perth's major strike lasted one month, in April and
May 1937, when Local 10 of the Canadian Shoe Workers and Allied Crafts
Union struck the Perth Shoe Co. Pickets and parades went up around town and
were described as orderly. The union, which represented 60 percent of the workers, wanted a closed shop, decent working conditions, and wages commensurate
with employees in other factories making the same kind of shoes. The company
had been dismissing union members, and relations broke down.[148]

It took A. R. Mosher, president of the All-Canada Congress of Labour, and
dominion conciliator M. B. Cambell to resolve the dispute, which saw wages for
trim work go up 2.5 cents an hour and 5 percent increases for piece work. However, the union failed to win the right to represent all the employees, and this
proved fatal. The firm split the work-force by creating, later in May 1937, the
Perth Shoe Company Employee Benefit Association, which offered non-union

members access to a social and recreation centre, a banking plan, and sick benefits, and sponsored euchre and bridge parties. On 3 July the association sponsored a picnic at Christie Lake.[149] By this traditional method, management attempted to buy employees away from union representatives. The scheme worked, and unions have had a minimal impact in Perth industrial relations. However, would the workers have received the benefits without the original challenge made by the union movement?

The Jergens Co. also kept unions out by being one step ahead of them. In 1925, it offered an annuity plan for retired salesmen; it extended the arrangement to all employees by 1930 and introduced group insurance and hospitalization plans for its largely female labour force.

The Rutherfords represent a tradition common in small-town industries. The family has worked for the Code Mill for a century. James Rutherford, a carder who died in 1908, was the first family member in the mill, followed by his son Jack, eight grandchildren, and a great-grandchild who is employed there yet. They worked at the upper mill, by Rogers Road (now demolished), or the lower mill, at Wilson and Herriott streets, For most of their years there was no union, just the familiarity of a stable job beside people they knew in the community, including the owners. Ron Rutherford worked 52 years for the mill and he lived almost as close to it as its original owner.

The Winn/Perth/Brown Shoe Co., Walmpole, Jergens, and Tayside Textiles offered local women wage labour. Women found themselves in an industrial setting, in manual jobs compatible with traditional perceptions of women's work (quality control, at sewing machines, in finishing sections, filling little bottles, applying labels, stitching pieces, sorting product) while men ran heavy machinery, carted, shipped, and managed. They were also hired because of their low wages (in 1907, men were paid $2.50-$3.00 and women $2.00 a week at Walmpole), although a second income in a family provided financial security not imagined on a single income.

Women were also partners and workers in various shops and businesses on the main streets, though seldom recognized as owners or proprietors. In the 1850s, widows Mary Quail, as proprietor of a Temperance Hotel, and Mrs. Wordie, as an innkeeper, carried on the businesses of their late husbands. Jane Laurie ran a bakery and confectionery for at least fifty years after being widowed. Several women ran businesses as milliners, dressmakers, grocers, druggists, and hotel proprietors. Anne Terney and Catherine O'Brien in succession ran a drug store from 1853 to 1873; Mrs. T. Reid, dressmaker, and Miss Fiddler, grocery-store owner, were active in the 1870s and 1880s. In the 1870s three grocery stores were owned and operated by women. Mary Morrison ran her own grocery at Mill and Gore streets from 1912 to

Meyer 'M. K.' Karakowsky and family, c. 1918. He arrived in Perth around 1910 from Russia, by way of Montreal, and he started a salvage and used goods store on Gore Street; his grandson "Benny K", kept the store into the mid-1980s. Post-1900 immigration brought multi-cultural diversity to Perth. Left to right, Rebecca (Hoffman), Meyer, Fanny, Zelda, Eli, c. 1918. (Courtesy Eli Hoffman)

the 1950s, and two sisters, the Mamie Grahams, ran a timeless candy store. Women were also listed in directories as musicians and schoolteachers, but never as homemakers or caregivers or as clerks and nurses. While wage labour in local industries altered old patterns of employment, it was not until after the Second World War that opportunities for women expanded considerably.

Immigration after 1900 introduced Perth to ethnic diversity not seen since original settlement. About 1910, Meyer "M. K." Karakowsky, a Russian, began a commercial venture in the "rag" trade which developed into a retail enterprise, known from 1939 until it burned in 1990 as Benny K's Surplus Store, after Meyer's grandson Benny. The store was described in 1955 as carrying clothes, plumbing, books, stoves, bicycles, horse hair, furniture, chick brooders, antiques, rags, and hardware.[150] Meyer's son-in-law David Hoffman went into business in 1928 and formed D. Hoffman and Sons; his sons Joe and Eli still sell a wide range of carpeting and flooring in an 1850s stone building next to the Benny K site on Gore Street.

Looking north on Foster Street toward Gore Street c. 1920s. Perth was a market town and administrative centre serving Lanark County. It was a business town of shops, general merchants, repair and maintenance outlets, commercial and professional services and with a limited but diverse manufacturing and industrial sector in the early 20th century. (Postcard, collection of author)

In 1908 Peter and Joseph Kanelakos from Greece began their highly successful enterprises on Foster and Gore streets. Peter ("the candyman") established a cigar store and billiard and shoeshine parlour; his enterprise was later taken over by O'Donnell Brothers. Joseph ran Palm Gardens confectionery, famous for its ice cream and sodas; it became Perth Tea Rooms by the 1930s, when purchased by another "candyman," Chris Moskos. The Moskos family started the Perth Restaurant about 1948. Howard Soong took over Hong Kong Cafe and produced his famous Chinese food at Harry's Cafe for decades, while German cuisine attracts a wide clientele at Maximilians dining lounge on Gore Street.

After several years experience in other towns, the Quattrochi and Rubino families, near-neighbours in Sicily, Italy, arrived in Perth in the 1920s and set up wholesale and retail outlets on Gore Street providing fresh produce year round through road and rail connections. J. Quattrochi and Sons and A. Rubino and Sons kept warehouses in Perth but established buildings convenient to railway lines in Carleton Place (Rubino) and Smiths Falls (Quattrochi). In 1946, the Quattrochis erected their own building on Gore Street; in 1950, the Rubinos linked up with IGA. Their stores expanded into groceterias. In 1960, Angelo

Rubino developed the IGA property on Wilson Street; the Quattrochis, feeling the pinch from the development of chain stores, concentrated by 1976 on wholesale. Phil Quattrochi moved to Kingston in the late 1940s to establish his own wholesale and retail network.

In spite of John A. Stewart's aggressive support of industrial development, Perth had only 3,790 inhabitants by 1920. From the turn of the century, however, Perth had been experiencing seasonal tourism which brought people to the region to visit local lakes and a town coming to be recognized for its quaint and picturesque qualities. The Rideau Canal, largely dormant as a commercial system, had come back to life in the 1880s as a source of recreation to an increasingly affluent middle class. Within the community and among vistors, boating, camps, cottages, and hotels opened a new horizon. Between 1899 and 1916, Perth serviced a line of small, dual-purpose steamboats that supplied and ferried the recreational community on the Rideau Lakes, as well as offering excursions on weekends, holidays, and moonlit nights.

Between 1921 and 1941, Perth grew by almost a thousand residents. Expansion by several industries such as Walmpole (1928), Perth Shoe Co.(1933) and Jergens (1938) boosted the manufacturing sector, although the Depression left scars. From 1901 the county population had been declining; not until 1961 did it climb above the figure for 1901, 37,232. This decline hurt commercial and supply outlets that serviced the agricultural community from Perth. Rural mechanization increased productivity but revealed the marginality of many local farms.

During and after the Second World War, Ottawa grew dramatically in both private and public sectors. Perth, 50 miles away, benefited from this expansion; branch plants considered its town bonuses and lower wage scales an advantage. J. A. Perkins, who transformed a car dealership into trucking and other commercial ventures, became president of the Eastern Ontario Development Association by 1955, and Glenn Crain packaged land deals for industrial and residential expansion. Perth's industrial parks attracted businesses such as 3M Canada, Aeroquip, Westinghouse Canada, International Silver, and Albany International, some of which have become mainstays in the local economy. Walmpole and Brown Shoes moved to new locations in Perth in the early 1960s, and Central Wire Industries Ltd. opened near North and Sherbrooke streets. Several diverse, small-scale firms now attract employees from beyond the town, and many Perthites commute as far as to Ottawa. Service industries and consultants have also found Perth convenient to regional and urban markets.

The irony of Perth's slow growth, yet stability, over 175 years is its wide recognition in heritage and tourist circles. Sustained growth tore other towns asunder. Tourism has become a major focus in Perth as a destination point. Despite peri-

ods of entrepreneurial neglect, Perth still maintains a diverse private sector and now proudly displays its distinctive character.

While manufacturing and small-scale industry were traditionally located on the perimeter of town, or by the river, they are now more clearly demarcated into development zones. From 1945, development along Dufferin Street or Highway 7, opened in 1932, allowed retail, service, and manufacturing outlets to expand. Perth annexed its first plot of land in over a century just north of the highway in 1952; opening of the Perth Mews Mall in 1990 symbolized growth along the thoroughfare. Improvements to the Rideau Ferry Road and Highway 43 to Smiths Falls helped pull Perth into the era of the automobile and the transport truck. The town annexed land for industrial parks from neighbouring townships, such as North Elmsley in 1969 and 1979 and Bathurst in 1980.

Gore Street c. 1900. It is one of the gems in small-town Ontario mainstreets. Its survival and revitalization is at the foundation of Perth's heritage profile. The Bank of Montreal building erected in 1884 is located second from the right while further down the street, the distinctive clock-tower identifies the Town Hall. (Postcard view, courtesy Canadian Parks Service, Rideau Canal Collection)

Within Perth, residential subdivisions such as Jamesville at George Street between Wilson and Drummond in the late 1940s and at Sunset Boulevard, Argyle Drive, and Inverness Avenue in 1962 predicted new growth. Land was annexed for Carsonview from North Elmsley Township in 1973 and for Perthmore Glen from Drummond Township in 1974. These residential areas absorbed homeowners working for local branch plants as well as commuters. Perth has also benefited from residential growth in neighbouring townships, especially in subdivisions located near scenic lakes and rivers and in ribbon development along roads near town. In the 1980s Perth experienced a boom in "adult life-style" condominiums, seniors apartments, new houses, and the restoration of old ones. The population of Perth stands at 6,000 and of Lanark County at 54,000.

Evolution and Change

With the construction of the first Tay Canal and later the Town Hall (1863) in the area reserved for the market on Cockburn Island, commercial activity had shifted down Gore Street to the Tay Basin. The cupola surmounting Town Hall focuses attention to this end of the street and signals the municipal anchor which at one time included council chambers, offices, meeting hall, jail, market, and, directly across the street, post office and library. Until the mid-1970s, this was the hub of downtown and anchor to the business district. Most people came here at least a couple of times each week to pick up mail, attend the market, pay taxes, or visit the library. At the same time they would frequent other businesses and purchase supplies. The chain holding the anchor broke when the post office began home mail delivery and then moved to a new building away from the core. It was further weakened when the library relocated after the building burned, in 1980.

Sprinkled along Gore Street are several fine brick facades; their corbelled surfaces and Victorian cornices add to the street's composition. The three-storey, dressed ashlar-faced Riverside building, backing onto the turning basin, is a fitting edge to development in the downtown core, and the McRae Block, directly across the river, is a classic Scottish piece. The hipped roof, recessed central pediment, and raised dressed quoins could be found on an Edinburgh street.

This streetscape proclaims the optimism and certainty of its times, as does the more flamboyant Darling and Pearson-designed former Carnegie library or "McMillan building," constructed nearly a century later in the Beaux-Arts style. Another notable building is the former Post Office (1930) across from the Town Hall; its clean lines, smooth sandstone finish, and austere styling sit comfortably with its Georgian neighbours. Further up the street, the Queen Anne-styled Bank of Montreal (1884) of Bathurst white sandstone adds to the rich legacy. Towering over all is the Gothic spire of St. James Anglican Church. Signature architects and landmark buildings are not uncommon in Perth. There was the Canadian Pacific train station (demolished) designed by the Maxwell firm of Montreal; the Anglican church by Fuller and Jones, and manse by King Arnoldi; and the wonderful crafts design for the Blair Funeral Home, 1937, by Edward Gardiner of the Ottawa firm of Burgess and Gardiner – each a statement of its era. Together they form a community of architecture which is Perth.

The story of evolution and change can be seen not only in the building styles but also in the changes caused by economic pressures. The Victorian shopfronts at Shaws and James Brothers were inserted along Gore Street in response to a shift in commercial traffic. Similarly the Art Moderne Perkins garage, on axis to Foster Street, elegantly heralds the automobile era. Only a few frame buildings remain in the commercial area; most were replaced over time in accordance with the business cycles of the town. One of the few remaining examples is 78 Foster Street: it started as a one-and-one-half-storey commercial outlet; it was converted during a building boom at the turn of the century to two and one-half storeys, and subsequently to a full three storeys. This phenomenon of adding floors, though not unique to Perth, was commonly undertaken; often the additions can be read as changes in material: different trim, window shape, or heavy Victorian cornices attached to earlier facades. Reading the changes to these buildings is a fascinating form of above-ground archaeology.

The central business district, which received a vital face-lift with the Heritage Canada improvements in the 1980s, is governed in part by the Business Improvement Association, formed in 1980. While tourist dollars gravitate to the centre of the old town, the commercial base is spreading outward. The Perth Chamber of Commerce (Board of Trade, 1890 to 1950), continues to play a key role. Although the Riverwalk project never got fully launched in the 1980s, the Tay Basin property remains an enticing challenge for an imaginative developer.

A view down Drummond Street toward the bridge, c. 1900. The plank sidewalk, dirt road and absense of hydro poles and wires would suggest an earlier photo except for the bicycle at left. The picture is taken in front of the stone wall protecting the Summit House. (Postcard, collection of author)

CHAPTER EIGHT

Community Endeavours

Entertainment

In the twentieth century, entertainment has come to symbolize a mass-appeal, global village phenomenon, absorbed through electronic media boxes stored in home entertainment areas. The city is avant-garde; town and country are folk. This narrow view of culture ignores the significant contribution made by local musicians, artists, and actors who are not satisfied with just watching and listening, but are inspired by doing.

The Perth Citizens Band is Canada's oldest town band, being formed in 1884. It had several antecedents. A band concert was given as early as 1855, and a St. Patrick's marching band played in 1867. In 1876, the local militia had a 42nd Battalion band, and in 1879 Professor Corrazzi conducted the Fire Brigade Band. By the 1890s, a Harmonica Band competed with the Citizens Band, and a bandstand was erected near the Tay Basin. In 1931 a new stand was put up behind the Town Hall, and in 1936 the Citizens Band played W. R. Spence's composition "Moonlight on the Rideau." Spence was the organist and choirmaster at St. James Anglican Church. The band provided jaunty airs for town parades, patriotic celebrations, excursion picnics, strawberry socials, civic holidays, visting circuses, and concerts in the park. It became part of the infrastructure of the town, an ambassador to other communities, and a source of local pride. It still practises every Tuesday evening above the fire hall.[151]

The Marks Brothers comedy and theatrical troupe had its origins nearby, on

Christie Lake, in the 1870s, and when they disbanded more than fifty years later – they had played before millions of Canadians and Americans. R. W. (Bob) Marks reportedly entered the entertainment business around 1876 by joining King Kennedy's touring magic act, "the mysterious Hindu from the Bay of Bengal." By 1879, Bob and Tom Marks began touring, and by 1890 – Mrs. R. W. (May A. Bell), George, Joe, Alex, Ernie, and Kitty were part of the clan that ran at least three companies that toured Canada and the United States until 1922.[152] Kitty Marks, who had her debut in the Perth Opera House, described the troupe getting under way:

> Tom and Ernie were the comedians of the family. The other three, Bob, Joe and Alex played it straight. All came directly to the footlights from their rocky pine-covered country on the shore of Christie Lake. Bob was a peddler when he took to the boards, untutored, but with enough savvy to learn quickly how to please bucolic Canadians of the last century. Ernie was learning the cheese-making business when he suddenly found himself on a stage without even having been coached on how to make a graceful bow. Tom abandoned his apprenticeship to a cobbler for the stage. Joe was within six months of his ordination to the ministry when he fell at the same time for the footlights and for Grace Andrews, a dim-

May A. (Bell) Marks acting in "Little Starlight" c. 1906. Kitty Marks remembered "the sight of a Marks troupe alighting from a train anywhere in the country sent a quiver of excitement through the station loungers equalled only by the excitement of a circus parade." (Courtesy Metropolitan Toronto Reference Library, Marks Brothers Collection)

The Marks Brothers Dramatic Company from Christie Lake near Perth, 1905: their troupe clockwise from left, Joseph, Thomas, Robert, Alex, Ernest, McIntyre and John became a national institution. They performed drama, comedy and vaudeville throughout North America from 1876 to 1922. (Courtesy Metropolitan Toronto Reference Library, Marks Brothers Collection)

pled ingenue with Bob's company. Alex, still on the farm, watched his brothers returning for summer holidays in plug hats, patent-leather shoes and diamond rings; then he too stamped the mud off his shoes and became an actor...[153]

Known as the "Canadian Kings of Repertoire," they brought to Canadian "opry houses" the latest London and New York plays and musical comedies. They introduced vaudeville-style acts to Perth audiences. Where regular tours by British and especially American theatre groups once dominated the local stage, the Marks Brothers adapted the standard melodramatic fare, full of virtue and villainy, for small-town audiences.

Each brother took his own company across the country for forty-two weeks a year before returning to Perth to rehearse and prepare new productions. Kitty Marks remembered appearing before audiences of all ages: "Playing to farmers who had hitched up in mid-afternoon to make their way over miles of treacherous roads just in time for the evening show, to school children who had been given a special half holiday to see a matinee, or to townsfolk arrayed in rustling crinoline and biting starch for a night at the 'opry house' made you feel you were fulfilling a mission rather than merely doing a job of work."[154]

The pinnacle of the Perth theatre tradition was the erection of the Balderson Theatre on Gore Street, which cost $150,000. It replaced the Starland Theatre,

Busy Gore Street, c. 1925. Banners suggest a special event, but Perth has a tradition of busy weekend activity. (Postcard, courtesy Rusty White collection)

located near the Tay Basin, and Nelson's Opera House. When it opened in 1915 with a performance by Kitty Marks, the building, with its opulent opera house decor, had a capacity ranging from 700 to 1,000 seats. Harry Houdini and many others once graced the stage and performed in an atmosphere that reminded visitors of the Winter Garden or the Royal Alexandra Theatre in Toronto. However, the favourite hometown Marks Brothers players were already declining, along with vaudeville acts and musical extravaganzas. Perth's live Marks Brothers gave way to the American Marx Brothers on film. The Balderson became a movie theatre with its first sound motion picture, shown in November 1930 – Eddie Cantor starring in Whoopee. Films began to displace live theatre, and by 1958, when the Balderson was closed, television had begun to make its impact.[155]

With the coming of radio and television, entertainment increasingly became a home activity; stars far from Perth invaded the local space where people used to make their own entertainment. The automobile further dispersed cultural activities. The annual Perth step dance and fiddling competitions are a throwback to earlier days when music from the old country blended with lyrics and tunes of the new. The Perth Community Choir, the Perth Summer Theatre (with some plays written by Perth's David Jacklin), the Unicorn Players, the Perth and District Drama Club, the Perth Performing Arts Committee, and spirited school productions are very active in sustaining and promoting music and theatre. Music thrives in several venues and styles, from choral to country.

Sports

When conditions were good, the Perth Basin was an excellent site for shinny. One pick-up game on a Sunday in 1930 brought Tay Canal bridgemaster McParlan, Police Chief Gilhooly, and Rev. Mckinnon of St. Paul's into controversy. McKinnon complained about hockey being played on the Sabbath and dispatched Chief Gihooly to disperse the rabble. Bridgemaster McParlan confronted the chief at the basin and told him to mind his own business, emphasizing that the Tay Canal was under his control and that he was well within his rights to attend to matters on government property. The issue was transferred to political circles, and McParlan and the hockey players were victorious.[156]

In the first season of the Perth Blue Wings juniors in 1936, coach Gene Chouinard and the team brought home the Ottawa Citizen Shield, and in 1938 they won the championship of eastern Canada, losing out in their quest of the Memorial Cup in the semi-finals. The Blue Wings still play in the Eastern Ontario Junior "B" Hockey League, where they were champions in 1991-92. Several graduates of Perth junior hockey have gone on to fame. Les Douglas was the first Perth man to have his name engraved on the Stanley Cup when the Detroit

Red Wings won in 1942-43. Hard-nosed Billy Smith played 15 seasons in goal for the New York Islanders, including four consecutive Stanley Cup winners 1979-83. He was on the first all-star team and won the Vezina Tropy for best goaltender in 1982, received the Conn Smythe Trophy for most valuable player in the playoffs in 1983, and shared the William Jennings Trophy for fewest goals against in 1983. Floyd Smith (no relation to Billy) played over 600 games and scored over 300 points in the National Hockey League for Boston, New York, Detroit, Toronto, and Buffalo between 1954 and 1972; he was head coach for part of the 1979-80 season and general manager of the Toronto Maple Leafs from 1989 to 1991.

In a town with a strong Scottish heritage, curling and golf have been popular. The Perth-Upon-Tay Curling Club was formed in 1875 and re-established as the Perth Curling Club in 1919. One of Canada's first ladies curling clubs was formed at Perth in 1903-04. Until the early 1950s, the men played with 60-pound curling irons (women with 30-pounders) before switching to Scotch granite curling stones. The Links O' Tay Golf and Country Club is the oldest golf course in continuous play in Canada. The first three holes were opened about 1890 on the old Matheson farm; cows and sheep stayed on as assistant groundskeepers. A local club rule allowed golfers to relocate their ball if it landed in "natural" soil.

Although not as well documented as organized sports, such activities as card playing, billiards, bowling, horseshoes and board games like parchese, chess, checkers, and crokinole were enjoyed in the community. Bowling and billiards were available in Perth at least as early as 1880. Lawn bowling was first introduced in 1927, and the open-air Perth swimming pool was launched on the Tay River in 1928.

Water sports and recreational boating were important in Perth, especially given the Tay River and nearby Rideau Lakes. A regatta in 1867 involved racing and a display of illuminated boats. An 1870 excursion on the Rideau Lakes launched William O'Meara's schooner, built at Oliver's Ferry; for 25 cents, participants could dance their way up to the Narrows and back. By the early 1880s summer camping and cottages were appearing up the Tay at Christie Lake, on Otty Lake, and around Rideau Ferry.[157]

The Second Tay Canal, begun in 1882, encouraged tourism. The canal reattached Perth to the Rideau system and its new-found recreational uses. Jacob Dittrick rented rowboats on the Tay before the canal was finished, and Sam Hall offered boats for hire at Rideau Ferry. Canal boat services operated by Peter Cavanagh advertised excursions and passenger service to the lakes in small steam yachts such as the *Katie, Swan, Aileen, Arrah Wanna,* and *St. Louis* between 1899 and 1916.[158]

The Meighen cottage on Rideau Lake, c.1930. Left to right, Florence Gould, Mabel Campbell, Morna Douglas, Gladys Ross, Ernie Meighen, and Stanley Ross. Built in McLean's Bay near Rideau Ferry in the 1870s it was the first of a wave of summer camps and dwellings erected by the Perth and Smiths Falls middle class on Rideau Lake. Improved roads, increased affluence, and more leisure time drew citizens to the surrounding lakelands. (Courtesy Stuart M. Douglas)

The opulent Edwardian cabin steamers *Rideau King* and *Rideau Queen* owned by the Rideau Lakes Navigation Co. provided full scheduled service on the Rideau Canal between 1900 and 1914; they used to visit Perth to conduct excursions on special days. Sixteen-year-old Fred Dickinson described his experiences on 15 August 1904:

As to-day was civic holiday in Perth, the masons there ran an excursion on the *Rideau King* away up the lake about 25 miles from the locks to Newboro.... The boat left Perth at 8 a.m. with 300 merry excursionists..we enjoyed the trip fine as the scenery on Upper Rideau Lake is magnificent. On the top deck the Perth Citizen's Band enlivened the crowd with music and on the second deck the piano and violin chimed together. Now and then we would meet a yacht and salute it. Again we would catch site of a family of loons swimming about near the boat and when we reached Rocky Narrows the fishermen could be seen hauling in the big salmon. The three of us climbed on the top deck where the band was and enjoyed the sun and wind.... At Newboro wharf the Brass Band of that place escorted the people up town.... While we were at Newboro the Perth Baseball Team played the Elgin team on the Newboro agricultural grounds. Perth was victorious and defeated Elgin by 13 runs to one.[159]

Sporting pressure on the Tay River's fish and foul stocks saw the initiation of the Angler's Association of Perth to protect the area and enforce fish and game laws. In 1909, a Mr. Gonyea of Perth started a sporting club that allegedly purchased the hunting and fishing rights from farmers whose land had been drowned by construction of the canal.[160]

Rideau Ferry became a summering adjunct to Perth, accessible by road or water. The Coutt's House Hotel, begun in 1881 and rebuilt in 1947 as the Rideau Ferry Inn, was a favourite site for picnics, outings, dances, and bands. A cottage cluster nearby became summer homes for Perth's emerging middle class. In 1897, the first annual Perth regatta was held at the Ferry on the civic holiday, attracting throngs of people. After the first gasoline-powered motorboat on the Rideau Canal was launched by carriage-maker Thomas Hicks and boat-builder Isaac Troke in the Perth Basin in 1901, the regatta picked up momentum as a racing venue. With motorboats all the rage, 41 craft were reported stationed at Perth by

The *St. Louis* in the Tay Basin, c. 1911. Between 1899 and 1916 Perth had a series of small dual-purpose steam yachts serving the Rideau Lakes recreational community. Steamers like the *St. Louis* delivered passengers and parcels and ran excursions to the lakes. (Postcard, courtesy Rusty White collection)

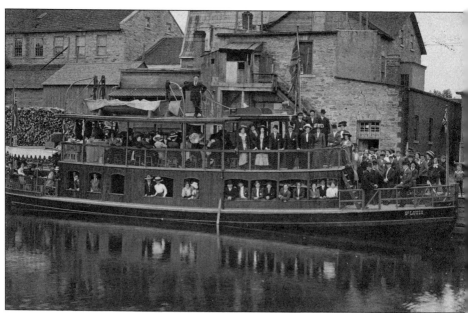

The annual Rideau Ferry regatta at the Coutts Hotel seen here in the 1940s. It was a hugely successful event for the first half of the 20th century, attracting thousands of visitors to this recreational extension of Perth on the Rideau Lakes. The event attracted professional boat crews in several motorized categories. (Courtesy Stuart M. Douglas, Smiths Falls)

1908. By the 1930s, the races at the Ferry involved special classes of boats such as those built by Myles Jeffrey of Athens, Ontario, as well as hotly contested international sea flea events. An estimated 10,000 people attended the 1937 regatta. Because of expansion of cottage areas and road access, as well as the portability of boats, the Tay Canal saw less pleasure boating, although the regatta continued to the early 1950s.[161]

Since the Second World War, the variety of sports available to Perth-area residents has mushroomed. Governments began to support leisure facilities. The old arena, with its beautiful wooden facade, was torn down by 1963; a community centre built in 1965 has an active hockey and figure skating program. The curling club is located in a structure erected in 1953. A pool was attached in 1975 to the John A. Stewart School, now home of the Perth Stingrays swimming team. Lawn bowling moved from the lawns of the United Church manse to the former site of St. Andrews Church. Perth's high schools still provide keen regional competition in several sports. The Perth Fairgrounds and local parks and schoolyards

The fertile clay plain around Perth sustained an important agricultural community. The farm of Ian Millar, near Jebb's Creek, is typical of the tradition. (Photo by Jayne Huddleston)

Ian Millar, world champion equestrian rider, with his faithful mount Big Ben. Millar came to symbolize tradition and style in Perth with the restoration of his farm and pursuit of excellence. (Photo by Jayne Huddleston)

offer venues for some activities, but the Conlon Farm recreational park, which opened in 1989, offers a first-class facility for baseball, soccer, tennis, basketball, and volleyball, as well as a children's playground.

If racing was one of the earliest sports at militia days and fairgrounds, horses in competition continue to give Perth world-wide recognition. Just outside town beyond Jebb's Creek, the Millar-Brooke Farm is the site of an excellent equestrian training ground. It is home base for five-time Olympic athlete, Pan American Games gold medal-winner, and World Champion show jumper Ian Millar and his equally famous horse, Big Ben. Millar has participated in many events with the Canadian equestrian team since 1971 and won the World Cup Equestrian Championships in 1988 and 1989 and the Du Maurier Ltd. International in 1991. At the Spruce Meadows National Show-jumping competition in June 1992 at Calgary, he became the first North American ever to achieve 100 Grand Prix career victories. In 41 of those victories, his mount was Big Ben.

Proud Traditions

On 20 August 1914, part of the 42nd Lanark and Renfrew Regiment marched proudly through Perth representing the first active service draft from that regiment. During the First World War, the regiment was transferred to the Canadian Expeditionary Force and contributed men to the 2nd, 21st, 38th, 77th, and 80th battalions. It also raised the 130th Lanark and Renfrew Battalion under Lieut.-Col. J.E. de Hertel in 1916 and the 240th Lanark and Renfrew Overseas Battalion. Men from the Lanark and Renfrew won battle honours at the Somme in 1916; Amiens and Arras in 1917-18; Hindenburg Line, Ypres, in 1917; and the pursuit to Mons. Many Perth and Lanark men were part of the 238th Forestry Regiment, active in supplying timber from French forests for several uses in the war, including supports for the front-line trenches. The war generated at home a massive volunteer effort, spearheaded by groups such as the Red Cross Society, which organized women to make clothes for the troops overseas.[162]

Kathleen Shaw of Perth won a Royal Red Cross Medal and was mentioned in dispatches from Field-Marshal Sir Douglas Haig while she served as a nursing sister with the Royal Canadian Medical Corps between 1914 and 1919. She spent gruesome years in casualty clearing stations, where the horrors of twentieth century warfare took their first toll, and she made 47 dangerous Atlantic crossings as matron on the hospital ship *Araguay*.

The Lanark and Renfrew Scottish Regiment served its militia function between the wars and used the armoury at the former Asbury Methodist Church after 1928. During the Second World War the regiment supplied many men for active service in several units and won battle honours at Coriano, Misano Ridge,

Casale, and Naviglio Canal in the Italian campaign. However, the complexity of modern war, requiring recruits for army, navy, air force, and specialties within, eroded the geographical orientation of some of the fighting forces. The 1st Battalion, Lanark and Renfrew Scottish, saw service in home defence, and a complete company of 250 officers and men was supplied to the Governor General's Foot Guards. Citizens of Perth contributed more dollars per capita to the war effort than any other town in Canada.

After the war, the regiment became the 59th Light Anti-Aircraft Regiment, Royal Canadian Artillery, but was later converted back into infantry and redesignated the Lanark and Renfrew Scottish. The regiment is currently affiliated with the Royal Highland Regiment (Black Watch) and is based in Pembroke. The militia still reflects a keen sense of local pride, and the regimental band is based in Perth as the Lanark and Renfrew Scottish Association Pipe and Drum band under the leadership of Brian Noonan. They play in military parades and at social events throughout eastern Ontario. The major focus in Perth at present for military tradition is the Perth-Upon-Tay Branch 244 of the Royal Canadian Legion, which has been located on the banks of the Tay Canal since 1966.

An active Gore Street, c. 1920s. Special wreaths and banners suggest a parade or special event. (Postcard, courtesy Rusty White collection)

CHAPTER NINE

Revitalization

Perth, with its architectural heritage, has carved a niche for itself as one of the most distinctive towns in Canada. Through preservation and revitalization, the old core of Perth and many of its residential and public buildings have helped define Perth's identity. The sense of awareness took time to grow, and the benefits have been widespread.

Little more than half a century after its origin, Perth was described as "the old historical town."[163] By the turn of the century, it was being recognized for its distinctive architecture. The Perth *Expositor* on 14 May 1896 reported: "the sinuous windings of the Indian trail have been supplemented by the fine streets and avenues, many of which, for beauty and general attractiveness are not surpassed anywhere."[164] The 1920 *Magazine of Progress* commented on its well-kept streets, "lavishly shaded and lined with stately public and business blocks and charming residences, models of architectural beauty...".[165]

Several publications rediscovered Perth's heritage fabric, sowing more seeds of imagination. In a section on Perth in *Rideau Waterway* (1954), Robert Legget wrote: "Modern storefronts face the broad roadway of the street; but above them the eye traces out with pleasure the fine lines of grey stone buildings reminiscent of Scottish architecture of the last century at its best. The elegance of the building now used by the Canadian Legion [Matheson House], for instance, would be typical of many older buildings, if only their trappings were stripped clean.... The genuine character and flavour of the past which have nevertheless survived all these unfortunate modernisms suggest that Perth, if reconstructed, might well be the Williamsburg of Canada...."[166]

Cruising the Rideau Waterway (1965), by Kenneth McNeil Wells, warned about "this old and busy little town, much spoiled by ignorant modernization of many of its century old buildings": "Perth is a strangely blind, almost perverse little town. It has yet to realize that what it has which is old is uniquely its own, that what it has which is new can be duplicated and sometimes excelled by any town, village, or city in the country. Perth does not guess that what the rest of the country envies it is not industry or its modernity, but its history, its fine old stone rimmed basin, its fine stone buildings, its antiquity, its old-world loveliness, those things in Perth, unconsidered and unvalued by Perth, which money cannot buy but which money can destroy."[167]

Several publications in the late 1960s stirred the pot. Stuart Wilson wrote "Gem of a Little Town" for the 1966 Habitat Conference in Montreal, published in *Perth Remembered* (1967). James Kinloch wrote in "Perth – Solidity and Style" in the *Canadian Geographical Journal* (August 1969), "for sheer interest as well as attractiveness, Perth itself might challenge any town in Canada, and find no takers."[168]

From the School of Architecture at the University of Toronto, Eric Arthur used to bring his students to Perth to record and draw its historic structures in the 1930s. The fire that burned half of the village of Lanark, and another at the Perth Hotel, both in 1959, raised Joni Mitchell's lament: "You don't know what you've got, till it's gone." In 1965, the near-destruction of the Matheson House lit the first spark of militant preservation interest in Perth. A movement led by Edward and Willa Shortt, Winnie and Cyril Inderwick, and Peter Code, among others, saved the house from the wreckers, and the Imperial Order of the Daughters of the Empire purchased it to be used as the Archibald M. Campbell Memorial Museum, or the Perth Museum. Fires in the Matthews block in late 1979 and the Carnegie library in January 1980 and the Code House later the same year hit three of Perth's most distinctive buildings. Instead of being torn down, they were rebuilt.

The School of Architecture at McGill University began to show interest in Perth. Professor Gordon Webber did sketchings in 1965, and an architectural exposition, "Perth Revealed," showed buildings on Gore and Foster streets as they would look if restored. In 1967, Project Perth was born, led by Ottawa's Alan Armstrong, executive officer of the Canadian Council on Urban and Regional Research. The architects of Ontario donated, as their Centennial project, the professional services of town planners Murray and Murray of Ottawa to prepare sketches revealing how buildings would look restored. Public meetings were held, and design clinics offered advice to property owners, aided by the Architectural Conservancy in Ottawa. Armstrong pleaded in "Perth Hereafter": "Every concerned person recognizes that literally no place on earth can match the coherent fabric and visible spirit of Perth at its best. If the established character of Perth were ever defeated or lost, there could never be another environment like it in the universe for all eternity." In 1974, the Perth Historic Preservation Committee of Project Perth presented "A Programme for Progress," calling for the hiring of an architect to study, conceptualize, sketch, and make plans for major renovations, especially on the main streets.[169]

Since the early 1970s, the growing preservation ethos in Ontario has been reflected in public policy and programs. Heritage foundations, architectural associations, business improvement districts, and planning agencies orchestrate a better understanding of needs and pressures. Over time, and not withstanding opposition, this ethos has permeated and melded into local by-laws and planning documents. In Perth, the town itself led this process. Although there was some local suspicion as to the ultimate ideals of heritage planners, especially over the fight to widen or save the Drummond Street bridge in 1979, much of the interest in revival came from within. In the 1950s, when a local planning board was established, it rejected proposals to develop commercial strips extending from Gore and Wilson streets. While some retail activity proceeded to Highway 7, the decision prevented the old core from dying. Beginning in 1970, the town assembled a block of land in the core for the express purpose of creating a downtown mall.

Passage of the Ontario Heritage Act in 1974 and creation of the Local Architectural Conservation Advisory Committee (LACAC) in Perth provided some leverage for protection, though the legislation's lack of teeth and ambiguity have at times proved frustrating. The Ontario Heritage Foundation (OHF) has provided advice and funding for restoration. The OHF and its parent body, the Ministry of Culture and Communications, have consistently been supporters and advocates for Perth. Working with LACAC and various property owners, they have reshaped the community's perception of its history. As owners of two of the town's most prominent buildings, they have set a practical example for care and management. The OHF received the McMartin House from an anonymous donor, and had been involved with its preservation in 1974 and 1975. A recent campaign has seen major repairs, including reconstruction of the original roof and construction of a rear service tower to provide universal access. With the death of Winnifred Inderwick, the foundation has initiated a preservation program for her home, Inge-Va, including repointing and repairs to the roof. Simultaneously it is working with the community to develop a feasibility study of its continued use and management.

The Perth Merchants Association and its successor, the Perth Business Improvement Association (BIA), formed in 1976, have played a major role in Perth's revitalization. The BIA has invested in beautification projects and provided a management structure within a defined area. In 1980, it joined with Heritage Canada to have Perth serve as a pilot Main Street project. This program sought popular understanding of preservation in the context of economic revitalization and increased awareness of and sensitivity to the cultural landscape. It has helped make the town a popular destination for tourists and other visitors. The key to the project's success was an on-site project manager. The program relied heavily on local participation and the skills of the manager to facilitate and encourage broad support. Most of the financial commitment was private, with seed funds coming from Heritage Canada, the Ontario Heritage Foundation, the Building Rehabilitation and Improvement Campaign (BRIC), and Parks Canada. Over the course of the project, property owners have invested heavily in building repairs, new construction, and beautification.

From its earliest days, Perth has attracted skilled artisans and craftsmen. One

Looking along the Tay Creek toward the back of the Matthews block on Gore Street. The river systems around Perth's islands have given character and variety to the downtown core. (Archives of Ontario, M. O. Hammond collection, AO 131)

Perth's 175th anniversary, 1991. The MacCulloch Dancers from Glengarry County do a Highland twirl during a parade. (Photo by author)

recent firm, Callender and Associates, designers and builders, blossomed briefly as a business and as a craft culture, providing training for designers, carpenters, and cabinet makers in restoration and traditional construction. During its heyday in the mid-1980s, it operated with a staff of 25, organized in three divisions: design, construction, and woodworking. The company attracted an amazing following but was not able to sustain itself. This endeavour focused attention on the demonstrated demand and need for specialized services in dealing with historic structures. It has brought about the establishment of a conservation program at Algonquin College, Lanark campus. Directed toward tradespeople and contractors, it is attracting students from across Canada. The building arts diploma program concentrates on carpentry, millwork, and masonry. Plans are under way to round out the curriculum with plaster and decorative arts.

Historical awareness in Perth has never been higher since the 150th anniversary of the Rideau Canal in 1982, the Haggart's Ditch Festival of 1984, Perth and District Collegiate Institute's "Raisin' the Devil" reunion in 1989, the Links O' Tay centennial of 1990, and the town's 175th "Come on Home" anniversary celebrations of 1991. The Perth Museum expansion under Doug McNichol has generated a dynamic new focus, and the OHF has a stake in both the McMartin and Inge-Va houses. Several buildings have received a major uplift as part of the revival. A whole new sector of services in Perth has developed around restoration and historical management, led by Heritage Canada's John J. Stewart, who entered the private sector as a partner in Commonwealth Historic Resource Management Ltd., now located in the Code Mill on Herriott Street. He and his partner, Hal Kalman, employ historians such as Larry Turner and conservation experts and heritage technologists such as Jamie Silversides, Ian Hunter, and Jim Graham. Perth is the base and inspiration for a nationally operated company specializing in historical research, design, and conservation.

Perth has more than architectural beauty; it has character of place. The quality of life has been strengthened by an ambience felt through the graceful harmony of its main street facades and the charming flavour of its residential streets and parks. Early in its development, Perth was portrayed as a paradise, and for many this still holds true. The historical spirit is an important part of Perth's identity, as well as of its economy. The first issue of *Canada Century Home* in 1983 described the town in "Perth Walkabout": "A first impression of Perth is that it is a wonderfully solid town. From the century stone buildings of the main street to the modern, flourishing industrial park, you respond to a town with a sense of purpose. And Perth is a pretty place too, with the River Tay branching and winding about creating islands in the centre of town. Like a ribbon around bouquets. Old stone bridges, balconies overhanging the stream, a tranquil park, smiling people – everyone's small town dream."[170]

Legacy and Loyalty[171]

Perth has been home for several remarkable businesses in all sectors of the economy. Some establishments have been in operation for considerable periods of time, some of which have had several different proprietors. These would include the Rideau Canal since 1832; the Perth *Courier* since 1834; The Perth Fair since 1845; Bank of Montreal since 1850; Shaws of Perth since 1854; Code Felt Ltd. since 1876; Links O' Tay Golf and Country Club since c1890; Sinclair Florists since 1891; James Brothers Hardware Store since 1892; Lanark Mutual Insurance Co. since 1896; Perth Community Care Centre (formerly House of Industry and Tayview Nursing Home), since 1901; Walmpole Inc. since 1905; Conway Men's Wear since 1907; Perth Planing Mill since 1908; Brown Shoe Company of Canada (formerly Winn Shoe Co. and Perth Shoe Co.) since 1911; Girdwoods Drug Store since 1911; Jergens Canada Inc. since 1917; Royal Bank of Canada and Bank of Nova Scotia since 1919; J. Quattrocchi & Co. since 1922; Great War Memorial Hospital since 1923; Dodds & Erwin Ltd. since 1923 (the Dodds side going back to 1870s); Burns Jewellers since 1925; Perth Museum, since 1925, Blair and Son since 1926; D. Hoffman and Son Ltd. since 1928; Dicola Fuels Ltd. since 1929; Perth Co-op since 1930; Donaldson's Shell since 1931; Moss Motors (formerly Craig Motors) since 1933; Barr's Esso since 1934; Canadian Tire Ltd. associate store, since 1938; Stedmans Department Store since 1939; Frontenac Packaging Ltd. since 1941; Sawdons Appliance Centre since 1943; McVeety Electric since 1945; and many more dating from the 1950s and 60s.

Some long serving establishments no longer in operation include Roderick

Matheson, general merchants, 1816-1870s; the Tay Navigation Company, 1831-1886; W. Northgraves & Co., watchmaker, jewellry, 1832-1900s; Farrell's harness shop, 1830s-1900s; Ferrier's harness shop 1832-1910s; McLaren Distillery, 1841-1916; Haggart flour mill, 1841-1913; Arthur Meighen & Bros., general merchants, 1848-1930; John Hart, bookseller, 1850-1928; Hicks Carriage Factory, 1855-1923; Rudd and Nielson, watchmakers and jewellry, 1850s-1930; Mrs. Jane A. Laurie's Bakery and Confectionery (famous for home-made Old English Stone Ginger Beer), 1858-1925; The Perth *Expositor*, 1860-1936; H. B. Wright and Son, Furriers and Tailors, 1860-1930s; Bothwell cooperage, 1860s-1900s; W. J. Pink furniture store and factory, 1874-1933; W. H. McIntyre & Co., photographers, 1880s-1927; McLaren's Bakery, 1875-1941; Harry's Cafe (formerly Hong Kong cafe), 1900s-1987; Perth Bottling Works, 1913-1964; Chaplin & Code, plumbing, 1919-1950s; R. A. Beamish Co. store, 1931-1984; Burchell Supply Ltd., 1936-1991; Perkins Motors Ltd., 1937-1990; Benny K's Surplus Store 1910-1991.

Other business locations can profess to have a lineage of similar operations at their sites for many years, including Blair and Son, a furniture business dating back on Gore Street through proprietors George Thompson and David Hogg to 1839, and the Perth Planing Mill on Wilson Street with its roots as Duncan Kippen's sash, door and blind factory originating in 1856; At the site of Girdwood's Drug Store on Foster Street there has been a pharmaceutical operation since the building was erected in 1871. Indeed a linkage exists between the present proprietors, the Newton family, back to a drug store on Foster Street in 1835. Likewise, the Perth Apothecary on Gore Street has roots as chemists and perfumers at the same building since 1858. At Code Felt Ltd. on Herriott Street, wool has been processed in some form or other since 1883. The most remarkable longevity for retail outlets is Shaws of Perth

In several trades, from artisans to professionals, Perth has witnessed long term loyalty and committment. Dr. James Wilson was a surgeon in Perth for 48 years, arriving from Lanarkshire, Scotland in 1821, just two years out of the University of Edinburgh, and returning to his native land in 1869 where he died in 1881. Wilson made an important contribution to the study of geology and perhaps lay the foundation of Perth's unique role of providing some of Canada's most famous geologists to the national scene, including Robert Bell and William Brock, both of whom headed the Geological Survey of Canada.

Long timers include Presbyterian Minister Rev. William Bell, 1817-1857; William Morris, Assemblyman, Legislative Councillor, cabinet member, 1820-1848; Daniel McMartin, lawyer, 1823-1860s; John Glass Malloch, Judge of the Lanark County Court, 1842-1873; Rev. William Bain, pastor at St. Andrews Presbyterian Church, 1846-1881; Thomas Brooke, town clerk, 1850-1894; James Bell, registrar of Lanark County, 1850-1910; Lanark County Sheriff James Thompson 1852-1893; Dr. John Kellock, physician, 1862-1898; and the Walker family ran the Perth *Courier* from 1863 to 1942. John G. Haggart served over forty years as Member of Parliament, 1872-1913; William Stevens Senkler, Judge of the Lanark County Court, 1874-1914; Francis Michell, Principal of P.C.I. 1875-80, Lanark County Inspector of Schools, 1880-1922; Dr. A. W. Dwyre, physician, 1885-1939; John A. Kerr, 40 years the town clerk; Rev. Dr. A. H. Scott (grandfather of champion figure-skater Barbara Ann Scott), pastor of St. Andrews Presbyterian Church, 1888-1926; Jim Gamble, firefighter and fire chief, 1897-1947; the Danner family managing and owning H. K. Walmpole Co. of Perth, 1906-1989; John Leo Walsh, dentist, 1923-1978; Murray R. Wilson, dentist, 1924-1974; J. A. B. Dulmage, lawyer, 1935-1985; John Mather, town clerk, 1943-1977.

Notes

NOTE: The Journals of William Bell are located in typed manuscript form at the Perth Museum, at Queen's University Archives, and in the Robert Bell Collection, National Archives of Canada. References are used here from all three sources. Only Volume 2, 1817 to January 1826, is in the form of true diary entries. All other volumes are journals written after the fact at a later date.

1. Marjory Whitelaw, ed., *The Dalhousie Journals* (Ottawa, Oberon Press, 1981) Vol. 2, p.42.

2. Glenn J. Lockwood, "The Pattern of Settlement in Eastern Ontario" *Families* Vol. 30, No. 4, Nov. 1991, p. 239.

3. H. J. M. Johnston, *British Emigration Policy 1815-1830* (Oxford, Clarendon Press, 1972) p. 16; J. M. Bumstead *The People's Clearance 1770-1815* (Edinburgh University Press/University of Manitoba Press, 1982) pp. 217-221.

4. Johnston, *British Emigration Policy*, p. 17

5. *Ibid.* pp. 18-19; See also "Liberal Encouragement To Settlers", Glasgow *Herald*, 27 Feb. 1815 (an original copy in Perth Museum).

6. Marianne McLean, "Achd an Rhigh: A Highland Response to the Assisted Emigration of 1815" *Canadian Papers in Rural History* (Gananoque, Langdale Press, 1985) Vol. V, pp. 181-185; Names of all emigrants in this migration are available in NA, MG 11, C0385, Vol. 2, "General List of Settlers...."

7. *Ibid.* p. 21; Jean S. McGill, *A Pioneer History of the County of Lanark* (Toronto, 1968) pp. 6-7.

8. NA, RG 5, A1, UCS, Vol. 25, p. 11, pp. 367-369, Petition of Scottish Settlers, 28 Dec. 1815.

9. Marianne McLean, *The People of Glengarry: Highlanders in Transition, 1745-1820* (McGill-Queen's University Press, 1991) pp. 196-201; see also McLean, "Achd an Rhigh", p. 186.

10. See Lillian F. Gates, *Land Policies of Upper Canada* (University of Toronto Press, 1968) pp. 85-92.

11. See "First Days" in Edward Shortt, ed., *Perth Remembered* (Perth, Perth Museum, 1967) p. 21; A comprehensive collection of documents on the Rideau Military Settlement is available in the Archives of Ontario, RG 1, A-1-7, Crown Lands Dept., Military Settlements, 1816-1818; 1818-1822; 1823-1835.

12 See J. D. P. Martin "The Regiment De Watteville: Its Settlement and Service in Upper Canada" *Ontario History*, March 1960.

13. "Swiss Regiments", *Perth Remembered*, pp. 25-27; Virginia Howard Lindsay, "Perth Military Settlement; characteristics of its permanent and transitory settlers, 1815-1822" Ottawa, Carleton University, M.A. Thesis, 1972, pp. 68-70.

14. William Dunlop, *Recollections of the American War* (Toronto, Historical Pub. Co., 1908) p. 61.

15. Perth *Courier*, 22 April 1921.
16. Rev. William Bell diaries in Robert Bell Papers, NA, MG 29, B15, Vol. 49, file 20, book 2, p. 70; See also Perth Military Settlement Book including register of location tickets, military settlers names and regiments, and other information in NA, MG 9, D8-27, Vols. 1 & 2. microfilm reel C-4651. Concerning the summer of 1816 see C. R. Harington, *The Year Without a Summer: World Climate in 1816* (Ottawa, Canadian Museum of Nature, 1992).
17. *Ibid.* pp. 41-47; see also Bell diaries typescript, Perth Museum, 24 June-9 July 1817, p.22-26.
18. Robert Gourlay, *Statistical Account of Upper Canada* (abridged by S. R. Mealing, Toronto, McClelland and Stewart, 1974) p. 273.
19. Interview with Mrs. Winnie Inderwick, Perth, "Ottawa Was Just Slabtown" in Joan Finnegan, *Some of the stories I told you were true* (Ottawa, Deneau, 1981) p. 63.
20. J. A. B. Dulmage, "Origins of the First Settlers" *Perth Remembered* pp. 22-24.
21. QUA, William Bell diaries, Vol. 4, 4 June 1826.
22. Hugh Halliday, "The Valley Regiments", unpublished manuscript.
23. Quoted in Richard Bonnycastle, *Canada As It Was, Is, and May Be* (London, Macmillan, 1864) Vol. 2, p. 107.
24. Thomas Fisher Rare Book Library, University of Toronto, Louis Melzack Collection, RB 154, 986, Broadside 'To the Inhabitants of the townships of Drummond, Lanark, Darling, Dalhousie, Bathurst, and North and South Sherbrooke, comprising the 1st and 2nd Regiments of Lanark Militia, Perth, 2nd November, 1838.
25. George Mainer, s.v. Matheson, Roderick, *Dictionary of Canadian Biography*, Vol. X, pp. 501-502. See NA, MG 29, E9, Percy Harold Gardner Collection for a history of the Lanark and Renfrew Scottish Regiment. See also *Regiments and Corps of the Canadian Army* (Ottawa, 1964).
26. Information on this section courtesy, the Hon. John Matheson, from a file on the guns kept at the Court House.
27. William Bell, *Hints to Emigrants*, p. 88.
28. W. H. Smith, *Canadian Gazetteer*, p. 144.
29. See Richard M. Reid, "The End of Imperial Town Planning in Upper Canada" *Urban History Review*, June 1990.
30. Perth Museum, Bell diaries typescript, 1819, p. 107.
31. J. K. Johnson, *Becoming Prominent: Regional Leadership in Upper Canada, 1791-1841* (McGill-Queen's Univ. Press, 1989) pp. 38, 70; Reid, *Upper Ottawa Valley*, p. 221.
32. Rev. James Ross, "Reminiscences of Perth by a Former Pastor", Perth *Courier*, 30 June 1905.
33. Gourlay, *Statistical Account of Upper Canada*, p. 276.
34. *Ibid.*, p. 359.
35. Perth Museum, Daniel Shipman broadside, 1824.
36. Lockwood, *The Pattern of Settlement*, p. 38; Lockwood, *Beckwith*, pp. 17, 18.
37. Quoted in Johnston, *British Emigration Policy*, p. 13.
38. *Ibid.* pp. 53-54; See Carol Bennett, *The Lanark Society Settlers* (Renfrew, Juniper Press, 1991); See also the office records of the Lanark Military Settlement, NA, MG 9, D8-16.
39. Quoted in Johnston, *British Emigration Policy*, pp. 54-55.
40. See Bruce Elliott, "Emigration from South Leinster to Eastern Upper Canada" in K. Whelan, ed., *Wexford: History and Society* (Dublin, Geographic Pub., 1987), also published in *Canadian Papers in Rural History*, Vol. VIII, 1992.
41. Gates, *Land Policies of Upper Canada*, pp. 92-93; Dulmage, *Perth Remembered*, pp. 22-24.
42. NA, MG 29, B15, Vol. 49, file 20, book 2, p. 48; Lindsay, "Perth Military Settlement", pp. 68-70.
43. Armine W. Mountain, *A Memoir of George Jehoshaphat Mountain* (Montreal, 1866) pp. 53-54.
44. Quoted in Reid, *Upper Ottawa Valley*, p. xciii.
45. J. K. Johnston, *Becoming Prominent*, pp. 175, 212, 220.

46. For information on the Boulton clan and their lifestyle see John Lownsbrough, *The Privileged Few: The Grange and Its People in Nineteenth Century Toronto* (Toronto, Ontario Art Gallery, 1980)

47. Perth *Courier*, 30 July 1869

48. William Cox, s.v. Radenhurst, T. M. *Dictionary of Canadian Biography*, Vol, VIII, pp. 732-734,

49. John A. Stewart, "Early Legal History of Bathurst and County of Lanark", Perth Museum, Perth Historical and Antiquarian Society Collection.

50. Perth Museum, Bell diaries typescript, pp. 179, 215.

51. *Ibid.*, p. 229; Edward Shortt, *The Memorable Duel at Perth* (Perth, Perth Museum, 1970) p. 8.

52. *Ibid.* p. 9.

53. *Ibid.* p. 7.

54. "The Duel of 1833 as recalled by Mr. Cromwell who was a member of the Wilson household at that time", typescript in the Perth Museum, Perth Historical and Antiquarian Society Coll.; See also Perth Museum, Bell diaries typescript, p. 257.

55. "Early Social Conditions" (handwriting would suggest authorship by Mary A. B. Campbell) manuscript on file at Perth Museum, Perth Historical and Antiquarian Society Coll.

56. Larry Turner, *The First Tay Canal in the Rideau Corridor 1830-1850* (Parks Canada, Microfiche Report Series 145, 1984) pp. 86-102.

57. Larry Turner, "The "Shinplasters" of W. & J. Bell, Perth, Upper Canada, 1837-1839", *The Canadian Paper Money Journal*, Vol. 22, No. 1, Jan. 1986.

58. Quoted in Johnston, *British Emigration Policy*, p. 21.

59. Robert Lamond, *A Narrative of the Rise & Progress of Emigration, from the Counties of Lanark & Renfrew, to the New Settlements of Upper Canada....* (Glasgow, 1821, facsimile, Ottawa, Canadian Heritage Publications, 1978); John M'Donald, *Narrative of a Voyage to Quebec, and journey thence to New Lanark in Upper Canada* (Edinburgh, 1823, facsimile, Ottawa, Canadian Heritage Publications, 1978); Rev. William Bell, *Hints to Emigrants; In A Series of Letters from Upper Canada* (Edinburgh, Waugh and Innes, 1824).

60. Perth Museum, Don McLaren Coll., Duncan Campbell to Peter McLaren, Caledonia, New York, 16 May 1818.

61. See Glenn J. Lockwood, "Irish Immigrants in the 'Critical Years' in Eastern Ontario: The Case of Montague Township 1821-1881" *Canadian Papers in Rural History* Vol. IV, 1984.

62. Extract from a letter of the Rev. G. J. Mountain written when accompanying his father, the first Bishop of Quebec, on his visitation of Upper Canada in 1820. Armine W. Mountain, *A Memoir of George Jesophat Mountain* (Montreal, 1866) pp. 53-54.

63. Edward F. Bush, *Overland Transport in the Rideau Region, 1800-1930* (Canadian Parks Service, MRS 424, 1979)

64. *Counties of Carleton, Lanark, Prescott, Russell and Ottawa Directory* (Montreal, Lovell & Co. 1884) p. 181.

65. Perth Museum, Bell diaries transcript, 27 Jan. 1826, p. 168.

66. An Act to Incorporate certain persons therin mentioned under the style and title of the Tay Navigation Company, Chap. XI, 1st William IV, 1831.

67. Ibid.

68. Larry Turner, *The First Tay Canal in the Rideau Corridor 1830-1850.*

69. Reid, *The Upper Ottawa Valley*, pp. lxxx-lxxxi.

70. Quoted in Douglas Hill, *Great Emigrations: The Scots to Canada* (London, Gentry Books, 1972) p. 85.

71. Reid, *Upper Ottawa Valley*, p. xxix; Census of Canada, 1871.

72. W. H. Smith, *Smith's Canadian Gazetteer* (Toronto, H. & W. Rowsell, 1846) p. 146.

73. Hilda Neatby, *Queen's University: Volume 1, 1841-1917* (McGill-Queen's University Press, 1978) pp. 15-17; see also H. J. Bridgman, "Three Scots Presbyterians in Upper Canada: A

Study in Emigration, Nationalism and Religion", Queen's University, PhD. Thesis, 1978.

74. Brockville *Recorder*, 26 May 1881.

75. "The means of education in the early days of the settlement of Perth", anonymous manuscript dated 12 November 1897 in Perth Museum, Perth Historical and Antiquarian Society Collection.

76. QUA, William Bell diaries, 14 July 1827, Vol. V, pp. 94-95.

77. Richard M. Reid, *The Upper Ottawa Valley to 1855*, pp. ccxxii-ccxxiii and ff. 23.

78. *Ibid.* cxix; Cutis Fahey, *In His Name: The Anglican Experience in Upper Canada, 1791-1854* (Ottawa, Carleton University Press, 1991) p. 39.

79. George F. Playter, *The History of Methodism in Canada* (Toronto, Anson Green, 1862) pp. 206-207.

80. Neil Robertson, "The Early Highland Settlement of Perth, Ontario", Sept. 1909, unpublished typescript in Ontario Archives, Alexander Fraser Collection.

81. Richard W. Vaudry, *The Free Church in Victorian Canada 1844-1861* (Waterloo, Wilfrid Laurier University Press, 1989) pp, 5-6.

82. Glenn J. Lockwood, "The Secret Agenda of the Upper Canadian Temperance Movement" in *Consuming Passions* (Ontario Historical Society, 1990) pp. 157-184.

83. Larry Turner, s.v. Bell, William Jr., *Dictionary of Candian Biography* Vol. VII, pp. 69-70.

84. Ontario Archives, Malloch diaries MU 842.

85. Larry Turner, "Alcoholism in a family 150 years ago" Perth *Courier*, 10, 17 Sept. 1986.

86. Lockwood. *Beckwith...* p. 196.

87. Bell diaries typescript, October 1829. p. 205

88. *Ibid.*, 10 July 1820, p. 101.

89. Rusty White Collection

90. Bell diaries typescript, February 1845, p. 423.

91. *Idid.* Nov. or Dec. 1844, p. 419.

92. Northern sections of Burgess and Elmsley north of the Rideau system were originally included in Leeds County in the Johnstown District, but were transferred to Lanark County in the Bathurst District in 1838; See Thomas A. Hillman, "A Statutory Chronology of Eastern Ontario, 1788-1981", *Canadian Papers in Rural History* (Gananoque, Langdale Press, 1984) pp. 305-308.

93. Perth Museum, Harper collection; Perth *Courier*, 21 June 1859; 23 Aug. 1872.

94. "A Visit to "Ye Ancient" Town of Perth, Ont." *Commercial Review*, 3 Aug. 1878.

95. H. Belden, *Illustrated Historical Atlas of Lanark and Renfrew Counties 1880* (Toronto, H. Beldon & Co., 1880, reprint edition, Port Elgin, Ross Cumming, 1972) p. 18.

96. *Ibid.*

97. Marilyn G. Miller, *Of Mines and Men, Small Scale Mining in the South Shield Region of Eastern Ontario 1850-1920* (Kemptville Regional Office, Ministry of Natural Resources, 1976) pp. 53-56; 65-76; 82-88.

98. G. M. Trout, "Mammoth Cheese" *Journal of Dairy Science*, Vol. XLIII, No. 12, Dec. 1960, pp. 1871-1877; Perth *Courier*, 20 Jan. 1899.

99. Perth *Courier*, 11 Oct. 1872; Perth *Expositor*, 18 May 1882.

100. Greg Kealey and Bryan Palmer, *Dreaming of What Might Have Be; The Knights of Labour in Ontario 1880-1900* (University of Toronto Press, 1987) pp. 70, 72, 77, 88.

101. NA, RG 43, Vol. 996, file 93926, Wise to Page, 3 Feb. 1882 (note on margin made 8 April 1882); Ibid., Vol. 2007, pt. 2, 8 Feb. 1882, pp. 101-103.

102. Larry Turner, *The Second Tay Canal in the Rideau Corridor 1880-1940*.

103. *Canada, House of Commons Debates*, Vol. XXXII, 54-55 Victoria, 1st Session; 7th Parliament, 12 Aug. 1891, p. 240.

104. Turner, *Second Tay Canal*, pp. 160-173.

105. Margaret Coleman, s.v. Cameron, Malcolm, *Dictionary of Canadian Biography* Vol. X, p. 124.
106. Perth Museum, Harper Coll.; Perth *Courier*, 14 Sept. 1849; Ian Clarke, *Motherwell Historic Park* (Parks Canada, Manuscript Report Series 219, 1977); QUA, Alexander Morris Coll.
107. Perth *Courier*, 25 Feb. 1881; 24 July 1903; 12 Nov. 1920; 13 June 1906; 26 April 1906; Perth *Expositor*, 5 March 1903.
108. Perth *Courier*, 23 May 1913; 18 March 1921; 16 Feb. 1906.
109. Perth Museum, Harper Coll.; Perth *Expositor*, 4 May 1922.
110. Rusty White Coll.; Perth Museum, Harper Coll.; *Commercial Review*, 3 Aug. 1878; Michael Taylor, "The Glory Years of Perth's Whiskey Kings", Perth *Courier*, 20 May 1987.
111. *Commercial Review*, 3 Aug. 1878; Toronto *Mail*, 14 May 1887; William Meighen obituary, Perth *Expositor*, 1 March 1917; "History of the Meighen and McLenaghan Families", undated typescript, Perth Museum.
112. *Commercial Review*, 3 Aug. 1878; Toronto *Mail*, 14 May 1887; Obituary of John Hart, Perth *Expositor*, 20 Sept. 1917; W. A. Newman, *Diary of a Voyage of John Hart of Perth, Ontario* (W. A. Newman, 1940); Incomplete selection of Hart publications available at Perth Museum.
113. Courtesy Alan E. James; Perth Museum, James Brothers Collection; Rusty White Coll.; Perth *Courier*, 14 April 1955.
114. See Richard M. Reid, "The End of Imperial Town Planning in Upper Canada", *Urban History Review*, June 1990.
115. Perth *Courier*, 27 July 1847.
116. Perth Museum, Mechanics Institute record book; "Prof. J. K. Robertson Relates Early History", Perth *Courier*, 29 Sept. 1955.
117. Perth *Courier*, 2 Feb. 1906; see also Norman Shrive, *Charles Mair: Literary Nationalist* (University of Toronto Press, 1965); Jean S. McGill, *Edmund Morris: Frontier Artist* (Toronto, Dundurn Press, 1984); Mary Fitz-Gibbon, ed., *The Diaries of Edmund Montague Morris: Western Journeys 1907-1910* (Toronto, Royal Ontario Museum, 1985); G. Simmons and M. Parke-Taylor, *Edmund Morris "Kyaiyii" 1871-1913* (Regina, Norman Mackenzie Art Gallery, 1984).
118. Perth *Courier*, 9 Nov. 1849; 23 July 1869.
119. Perth Museum, Perth Historical and Antiquarian Society Collections, "Music and Musicians" by Anna M. Allan, 10 Dec. 1897.
120. Bell diaries typescript, May, 1829, p. 200.
121. Donald Fraser, "The Old Fire Companies", Perth *Courier*, 30 June 1905.
122. James Kinloch, "Sporting Days" *Perth Remembered* pp. 122-124.
123. Rusty White Collection
124. Quoted in Gordon W. Wilson and George M. Richardson, *A History of St. Paul's United Church and its Antecedents in Perth 1817-1975* (Perth, St. Paul's United Church, 1975) p. 9
125. Ontario Archives, Bell Papers, MU 7098, B-2, part of a seven page printed letter to the Rev. William Bell from 'a Presbyterian', undated.
126. See Vaudry, *The Free Church in Victorian Canada*.
127. Ontario Archives, Alexander Fraser Coll.
128. Westfall, *Two Worlds*, pp. 19-48; 83-84; Fahey, *In His Name*, p. 275.
129. Marion McRae and Anthony Adamson, *Hallowed Walls: Church Architecture in Upper Canada* (Toronto, Clarke, Irwin & Co., 1975) p. 135.
130. William Westfall, *Two Worlds: The Protestant Culture of Nineteenth Century Ontario* (McGill-Queen's Press, 1989) pp. 9, 40, 75, 127.
131. Perth Museum, Harper Coll.
132. J. E. Wells, *Life and Labors of Robert Alex. Fyfe, D.D.* (Toronto, W. J. Gage, n.d.) pp. 93-105; J. W. Grant, *A Profusion of Spires: Religion in Nineteenth-Century Ontario* (University of Toronto Press, 1988) p. 160.
133. Wilson and Richardson, *St. Paul's Church*.

134. C. K. Sissons, *John Kerr* (Toronto, Oxford University Press, 1946) p. 13.

135. "P&DCI Special Commemorative Issue 1989 Reunion", Perth *Courier*, 5 July 1989; See also James Kinloch, "The Collegiate Institute", *Perth Remembered*, pp. 151-154.

136. Sister Mary Berna, "St, John's Separate School", *Perth Remembered*, p. 82.

137. Perth *Courier*, 30 Aug. 1951; Perth Museum, Harper Coll.

138. Perth Museum, Harper Coll.; George F. G. Stanley, *Toil and Trouble: Miltary Expeditions to Red River* (Ottawa, Canadian War Museum, 1989) p. 151; C. K. Sissons, *John Kerr* (Toronto, Oxford University Press, 1946).

139. Charles Pelham Mulvaney, *The History of the North-West Rebellion of 1885* (Toronto, A. H. Hovey, 1886) pp. 231-234.

140. Perth Museum, undated.

141. J. K. Robertson, *Tayville* (Toronto, Ryerson Press, 1932) pp. 102-103.

142. *Ibid.* p. 97.

143. Perth *Courier*, 30 June 1905.

144. Perth *Expositor*, 12 Oct. 1922; Perth *Courier*, 14 May 1965.

145. Rusty White Coll.; "John Stewart's Empire" Perth *Courier*, 14 May 1965.

146. Perth *Expositor*, 26 March 1903; Rusty White Coll.

147. Perth *Expositor*, 12 Oct. 1922.

148. Perth *Courier*, 30 April, 14 May, 1937.

149. *Ibid.* 28 May, 9 July 1937.

150. Perth *Courier*, 9 June 1955.

151. Courtesy Peter Code; Rusty White Collection; Maureen Pegg, "Citizen's Band", Perth *Courier*, 17 June 1992.

152. Ann Saddlemeyer, ed., *Early Stages: Theatre in Ontario 1800-1914* (University of Toronto Press, 1990) pp. 48, 127, 325, 327.

153. Kitty Marks with Frank Croft, "My Life With the Marks Brothers" *Perth Remembered*, pp. 113-114.

154. *Ibid.* p. 115.

155. Perth Museum, Harper Collection; Perth *Courier*, 7 June 1978.

156. Larry Turner, *The Second Tay Canal in the Rideau Corridor*, pp. 171-172.

157. Perth *Courier*, 2 Aug. 1870.

158. Turner, *Second Tay Canal*, p. 214.

159. Fred Dickinson diary, copies at Archives of Ontario and Rideau Canal Office, Smiths Falls.

160. NA, RG 43, B61, Vol. 2015 pt. 2, pp. 256,7, Phillips to Jones, 16 Sept. 1909.

161. Turner, *Recreational Boating*; Perth *Courier*, 30 July 1937.

162. Michael Taylor, "The Lanark and Renfrew Scottish Regiment", Perth *Courier*, 20 Aug. 1986.

163. *Commercial Review*, 3 Aug, 1878.

164. Perth *Expositor*, 14 May 1896.

165. *Magazine of Progress*, 1920.

166. Robert Legget, *Rideau Waterway* (University of Toronto Press, 1955) p. 138.

167. K. M. Wells, *Cruising the Rideau Waterway* (Toronto, McClelland and Stewart, 1965) p. 55.

168. *Perth Remembered*; James Kinlock, "Perth-Solidity and Style", *Canadian Geographical Journal*, August 1969, p. 51.

169. Kinloch, "Perth-Solidity and Style", p. 41; Ottawa *Journal*, 3 Feb. 1967; *Perth Remembered*, pp. 172-173.

170. "Perth Walkabout", *Canada Century Home*, March-April 1983, p. 25.

171. Information from various historical directories; Rusty White Coll.; Perth Museum, Harper Coll.; special trade editions: *Commercial Review*, 3 Aug. 1878; Toronto *Mail*, 14 May 1887; Perth *Expositor*, 14 May 1896; taped interviews and courtesy several Perth businesses.

Bibliography

Primary Sources

Archives of Ontario
Crown Lands Papers, Rideau Military Settlement
Alexander M. Campbell Collection
W.T.L. Harper Reminiscences
Alexander Morris Papers
Journal of John Glass Malloch
Bell Family Papers
C.J. Foy Papers
Thomas Radenhurst Papers

National Archives of Canada
British Colonial Office and War Office Records on microfilm
Archibald M. Campbell Papers
Robert Bell Papers
Howard Morton Brown Collection
Perth Military Settlement
Lanark Military Settlement
Moffatt Family Papers
Edmund Montague Morris Papers
Percy Harold Gardner Collection

Perth Museum
Bathurst (Perth) *Courier* (1834-) on microfilm
Hart Almanac, 1860, 1866, 1874, 1913, 1914
Inderwick Collection
Perth *Expositor* (1860-1936) on microfilm
Perth Historical and Antiquarian Society Papers

Radenhurst Papers
W. T. L. Harper Collection

Queen's University Archives
William Bell Papers and Journals
William Morris Papers
Lockwood Collection

University of Toronto, Fisher Rare Book Library
Louis Melzack Collection

Books

Akenson, Donald H. *The Irish in Ontario: A Study in Rural History*. Montreal and Kingston, McGill-Queen's Press, 1984.

Belden, H. *Illustrated Historical Atlas of Lanark and Renfrew Counties 1880*. Toronto, H. Belden, 1880, reprinted, Port Elgin, Ross Cumming, 1972.

Bell, Rev. William. *Hints to Emigrants; In A Series of Letters From Upper Canada*. Edinburgh, Waugh and Innes, 1824.

Bennett, Carol. *The Lanark Society Settlers*. Renfrew, Juniper Press, 1991.

Brown, Horace M. *The Lanark Legacy: Nineteenth Century Glimpses of an Ontario County*. Corporation of the County of Lanark, 1984.

Bumstead, J. M. *The People's Clearance 1770-1815*. Winnipeg, University of Manitoba Press, 1982.

Careless, J.M.S. *The Union of the Canadas: The Growth of Canadian Institutions*. Toronto, McClelland and Stewart, 1967.

Craig, Gerald M. *Upper Canada: The Formative Years, 1784-1841*. Toronto, McClelland and Stewart, 1963.

Elliott, Bruce. *Irish Migrants in the Canadas: A New Approach*. Montreal and Kingston, McGill-Queen's Press, 1989.

Fahey, Curtis. *In His Name: The Anglican Experience in Upper Canada, 1791-1854*. Ottawa, Carleton University Press, 1991.

Gates, Lillian. *Land Policies of Upper Canada*. Toronto, University of Toronto Press, 1968.

Gourlay, Robert. *Statistical Account of Upper Canada*. 1822, abridged with a new introduction by S. R. Mealing, Toronto, McClelland and Stewart, 1974.

Grant, John Webster. *A Profusion of Spires: Religion in Nineteenth-Century Ontario*. Toronto, University of Toronto Press, 1988.

Hart, John. *Diary of a Voyage of John Hart of Perth, Ontario*. W. A. Newman, 1940.

Haydon, Andrew. *Pioneer Sketches of the District of Bathurst*. Toronto, 1925.

Hill, Douglas. *Great Emigrations: The Scots to Canada*. London, Gentry Books, 1972.

Johnson, J. K. *Becoming Prominent: Regional Leadership in Upper Canada, 1791-1841*. Montreal and Kingston, McGill-Queen's Press, 1989.

Johnston, H. J. M. *British Emigration Policy 1815-1830: Shovelling Out Paupers*. Oxford, Clarendon Press, 1972.

Kealey, Greg and Bryan Palmer. *Dreaming of What Might Be: The Knights of Labour in Ontario 1880-1900*. Toronto, New Hogtown Press, 1987.

Lamond, Robert. *A Narrative of the Rise & Progress of Emigration, from the Counties of Lanark & Renfrew, to the New Settlements of Upper Canada...* Glasgow, 1821, facsimile, Ottawa, Canadian Heritage Publications, 1978.

Legget, Robert. *The Rideau Waterway*. Toronto, University of Toronto Press, 1956.

Lockwood, Glenn J. *Beckwith: Irish and Scottish Identities in a Canadian Community 1816-1991*. Corporation of the Township of Beckwith, 1991.

MaCrae, Marion and Anthony Adamson. *The Ancestral Roof: Domestic Architecture of Upper Canada*. Toronto, Clarke, Irwin & Co., 1963.

MaCrae, Marion and Anthony Adamson. *Hallowed Walls: Church Architecture of Upper Canada*. Toronto, Clarke, Irwin & Co., 1975.

M'Donald, John. *Narrative of a Voyage to Quebec, and journey thence to New Lanark in Upper Canada*. Edinburgh, 1823, facsimile, Ottawa, Canadian Heritage Publications, 1978.

McGill, Jean S. *A Pioneer History of the County of Lanark*. Toronto, 1968.

McGill, Jean S. *Edmund Morris: Frontier Artist*. Toronto, Dundurn Press, 1984.

McKenzie, Ruth. *A History of Leeds and Grenville County*. Toronto, University of Toronto Press, 1967.

McLean, Marianne. *The People of Glengarry: Highlanders in Transition, 1745-1820*. Montreal and Kingston, McGill-Quenn's University Press, 1991.

Millar, Ian and Larry Scanlan. *Riding High: Ian Millar's World of Show Jumping*. Toronto, McClelland and Stewart, 1990.

Mountain, Armine W. *A Memoir of George Jehoshaphat Mountain*. Montreal, 1866.

Neelin, James M. and Michael R. *The Old Methodist Burying Grond in the Town of Perth, Lanark County, Ontario*. Ottawa Branch, Ontario Genealogical Society, 1979.

Osborne, Brian S. and Donald Swainson. *Kingston: Building on the Past*. Westport, Butternut Press, 1988.

Playter, George F. *A History of Methodism in Canada*. Toronto, Anson Green, 1862.

Reid, Richard M. *The Upper Ottawa Valley to 1855*. Ottawa, Carleton University Press, 1990.

Reid, Stanford W., ed. *The Scottish Tradition in Canada*. Toronto, McClelland and Stewart, 1976.

Richardson, Douglas et. al. *Ontario Towns*. Toronto, Oberon Press, 1974

Robertson, John Kellock. *Tayville*. Toronto, Ryerson Press, 1932.

Saddlemeyer, Ann, ed. *Early Stages: Theatre in Ontario 1800-1914*. Toronto, University of Toronto Press, 1990.

Sissons, Constance Kerr. *John Kerr*. Toronto, Oxford University Press, 1946.

Shortt, Edward ed. *Perth Remembered*. Perth, The Perth Museum, 1967.

Shortt, Edward. *The Memorable Duel at Perth*. Perth, The Perth Museum, 1970.

Shrive, Norman. *Charles Mair: Literary Nationalist*. Toronto, University of Toronto Press, 1965.

Skelton, Isabel. *A Man Austere: William Bell*. Toronto, Ryerson Press, 1947.

Smith, Josephine. *Perth-on-the-Tay: A Tale of Transplanted Highlanders*. Ottawa, 1901, reprinted, Prescott, M. R. Livingston, 1987.

Souvenir, Old Home Week June 29th to July 5th, 1925, Perth. Perth, The Perth Expositor Print, 1925.

Souvenir, Perth Old Home Week, June 27th to July 4th, 1948. Perth, The Courier Pub. Co., 1948.

Sutherland, Lloyd C. *Yearning For Learning: The Story of Education in Lanark County 1804-1867.* Toronto, 1979.

Vaudry, Richard W. *The Free Church in Victorian Canada 1844-1861.* Waterloo, Wilfrid Laurier University Press, 1989.

Walker, Harry and Olive. *Carleton Saga.* Ottawa, Runge Press, 1968

Wells, J. E. *Life and Labors of Robert Alex. Fyfe, D. D.* Toronto, W. J. Gage, n.d.

Wells, Kenneth McNeil. *Cruising the Rideau Waterway.* Toronto, McClelland and Stewart, 1965.

Wilson, Gordon Weir and George M. Richardson. *A History of St. Paul's United Church and Its Antecedents in Perth, 1817-1975.* The United Church of Canada, 1975.

Westfall, William. *Two Worlds: The Protestant Culture of Nineteenth Century Ontario.* Kingston and Montreal, McGill-Queen's University Press, 1989.

Articles

Bruce Elliott. "Emigration from South Leinster to Eastern Upper Canada". *Wexford: History and Society.* Kevin Whelan, ed., Dublin, Geographic Pub., 1987.

Joan Finnegan. "Ottawa was just slabtown", Mrs. Winnie Inderwick, Perth" in Finnegan, ed., *Some of the stories I told you were true.* Ottawa, Deneau Pub., 1981.

George Galt. "Perth Revival: Dramatic mainstreet program has restored a small Ontario town's charm and character". *Canadian Geographical Journal,* Vol. 104, No. 4, Aug.-Sept. 1984.

"The Haggarts". *Historical Sketches of Ontario.* Toronto, Ontario Ministry of Culture and Recreation, n.d.

Thomas A. Hillman. "A Statutory Chronology of Eastern Ontario 1788-1981". *Canadian Papers in Rural History,* Vol. IV, 1984.

Glenn, J. Lockwood. "Irish Immigrants and the "Critical Years" in Eastern Ontario: The Case of Montague Township 1821-1881". *Canadian Papers in Rural History,* Vol. IV, 1984.

Glenn J. Lockwood. "The Secret Agenda of the Upper Canadian Temperance Movement". *Consuming Passions,* Ontario Historical Society, 1990.

Glenn J. Lockwood. "The Pattern of Settlement in Eastern Ontario". *Families,* Vol. 30, No. 4, Nov. 1991.

James Kinloch. "Perth- Solidity and Style". *Canadian Geographical Journal.* Aug. 1969.

J.D.P. Martin. "The Regiment De Watteville: Its Settlement and Service in Upper Canada". *Ontario History,* March 1960.

Marianne McLean. "Achd an Rhigh: A Highland Response to the Assisted Emigration of 1815". *Canadian Papers in Rural History,* Vol. V, 1985.

H. R. Morgan. "The first Tay Canal, an abortive Upper Canadian transportation enterprise of a century ago". *Ontario History,* Vol. 29, 1933.

Diane Newell. "Two Early Perth Houses". *Canadian Collector.* July/Aug. 1975.

"Perth Walkabout". *Canada Century Home*, No. 1, Mar.-Apr. 1983

Richard M. Reid. "The End of Imperial Town Planning in Upper Canada". *Urban History Review,* June 1990.

Richard M. Reid. "The Reverend William Bell: One Emigrant's Adjustments to Upper Canada". *Scottish Tradition.* Vol. 10, 1979-80.

Michael Taylor. "The glory years of Perth's Whiskey Kings". Perth *Courier,* 20 May 1987.

Michael Taylor. "The Lanark and Renfrew Scottish Regiment". Perth *Courier,* 20 Aug. 1986.

Michael Taylor. "Perth Industries that have passed into time". Perth *Courier,* 21 Sept. 1988.

Larry Turner. "Alcoholism in a family 150 years ago". Perth *Courier,* 10, 17 Sept. 1986.

Larry Turner. "The Merchant Notes of W.& J. Bell, Perth, Upper Canada". *Canadian Paper Money Journal,* Vol. 22, No. 1, Jan. 1986.

Articles in the Dictionary of Canadian Biography:

Watteville, Louis De (1776-1836) by Rene Chartrand, Vol. 6, pp. 896-9. Bell, William jr. (1806-1844) by Larry Turner, Vol. 7, pp. 69-70. Thom, Alexander (1775-1845) by Charles G. Roland. Vol. 7, pp. 852,3. Bell, William (1780-1857) by H.J. Bridgman, Vol. 8, pp.76,7. Morris, William (1786-1858) by H.J. Bridgman, Vol. 8, pp.638-42. Radenhurst, Thomas M. (1803-1854) by William Cox, Vol. 8, pp. 732-4. Cameron. Malcolm (1808-1876) by Margaret Coleman, Vol. 10, pp.124-9. Matheson, Roderick (1793-1873) by Geo. Manier, Vol. 10, pp. 501,2.

Theses and Reports

Bridgman, H.J. "Three Scots Presbyterians in Upper Canada: A Study in Emigration, Nationalism and Religion". Queen's University, Ph D. Thesis, 1978.

Crerar, Duff W. "Church and Community: The Presbyterian Kirk-Session in the District of Bathurst". University of Western Ontario, M.A. Thesis, 1979.

Halliday, Hugh. "The Valley Regiments". Unpublished manuscript.

Lindsay, Virginia L. "Perth Military Settlement: characteristics of its permanent and transitory settlers, 1816-1822". Carleton University, M.A. Thesis, 1972.

Lockwood, Glenn J. "Eastern Ontario Perceptions of Irish Immigrants, 1824-1868". University of Ottawa, Ph D. Thesis, 1987.

Sneyd, Robert B. "The Role of the Rideau Waterway". University of Toronto, M.A. Thesis, 1965.

Turner, Larry. The First Tay Canal in the Rideau Corridor, 1830-1850. Parks Canada, Microfiche Report Series 145, 1984.

Turner, Larry. The Second Tay Canal in the Rideau Corridor, 1880-1940. Parks Canada, Microfiche Report Series 295, 1986.

Turner, Larry. Recreational Boating on the Rideau Waterway, 1890-1930. Parks Canada, Microfiche Report Series, 253, 1985.

Index

ABOUT THE AUTHORS

LARRY TURNER has been compiling a
data bank on Perth for more than fif-
teen years and is principal historian of
Commonwealth Historic Resource
Management of Perth and Vancouver.
A graduate in history from Trent and
Queen's universities, he is the author
of *Voyage of a Different Kind: The Associated Loyalists of Kingston and Adolphus-
town* (1984) and co-editor of *On a Sunday Afternoon: Classic Boats on the
Rideau Canal* (1989), as well as several
other articles, reports and biographies
of individuals, places and events in
Eastern Ontario. He is currently Chairman of the Friends of the Rideau.

JOHN J. STEWART galvanized the revival
of Perth as the head of Heritage Canada's
Main Street Programme from 1980 to

Larry Turner (right) and John J. Stewart.
(Photo by Maureen Pegg, *Perth Courier*)

1984. A landscape architect by profession, he charted a path by which businesses
and residents could revive their downtown character. With his longstanding interest in Perth architecture, he shares with many others a commitment to Perth's
preservation and continued vitality. His research into Perth's stonemasons,
quarry locations, local trades and artisans provides insights into the town's built
heritage. In 1984 he founded a partnership, Commonwealth Historic Resource
Management Limited, with offices in Perth and Vancouver. He is a former member of LACAC and currently chairs the Perth Museum Board.